Good Date, Bad Date

Also by Marla Martenson

Excuse Me, Your Soul Mate Is Waiting

Good Date, Bad Date

The Matchmaker's Guide to Where the Boys Are — and How to Get Them

MARLA MARTENSON

HAMPTON ROADS
PUBLISHING COMPANY, INC.

The names and background information of the people in
this book have been changed to protect their identities.

Cover design by Laura Beers
Cover art illustration © CSA Images

Hampton Roads Publishing Company, Inc.
1125 Stoney Ridge Road
Charlottesville, VA 22902

434-296-2772
fax: 434-296-5096
e-mail: hrpc@hrpub.com
www.hrpub.com

If you are unable to order this book from your local
bookseller, you may order directly from the publisher.
Call 1-800-766-8009, toll-free.

Library of Congress Cataloging-in-Publication Data

Martenson, Marla.
 Good date, bad date : the matchmaker's guide to where the boys are and how
to get them / Marla Martenson.
    p. cm.
 Summary: "Another dating guide from Beverly Hills-matchmaker Marla
Martenson, this book specifically targets women to show them how to get a
man and how to keep him"--Provided by publisher.
 ISBN 978-1-57174-600-9 (5.5 x 8.5 tp : alk. paper)
 1. Mate selection. 2. Dating (Social customs) I. Title.
HQ801.M3734 2009
646.7'7082--dc22

2008050408

ISBN 978-1-57174-600-9
10 9 8 7 6 5 4 3 2 1
Printed on acid-free paper in the United States

This book is dedicated to my soul mate and husband, Adolfo Bringas. I am so grateful to have my best friend at my side to go through life with. And to my beloved mother, Donna Reed, for her support and being my biggest fan.

Contents

Introduction

Love is the most powerful force in the universe. Every single one of us longs to love and be loved in return by that special soul mate. No matter how many bad relationships we suffer through, how many disastrous dates we go on, or what painful divorces we survive, our hearts never give up on finding "the one." In my first book, *Excuse Me, Your Soul Mate Is Waiting,* I outlined four simple steps to harness the power of attraction and take control of your love life. The goal was to empower my readers so that they would be fully prepared and in the right frame of mind not only to expect but also to find the love of their lives!

But even when you find that one true love, life doesn't just fall neatly into place. Getting to truly know someone and be sure they are "the one" is a process fraught with pitfalls. I know—in my job as a professional matchmaker I've seen them all. I know that a lucky few of you readers actually enjoy the dating process. You find it a lot of fun to get out there and meet new people. Some women love the idea of being wined, dined, and pampered, and truly enjoy the experience of meeting new men. Many others absolutely dread the very thought of "dating." These women would rather stay home and watch another rerun of *Mister Ed* on Nick at Nite than endure yet another disappointing blind date.

But of course you know that the possibility of Mr. Right knocking on your door is extremely low. Unless you happen to fall in love with the UPS deliveryman, cable guy, or plumber who comes over to unclog your kitchen sink, then you have to get out there—at least a little bit!—to up your chances of meeting someone. Whether you like the idea of dating or dread it, at some point you will most likely surrender to it. And guess what? Dating is a skill that can be developed like any other. Jumping in blindly with no game plan can be downright disastrous, not to mention frustrating and time-consuming. A string of bad dates and misunderstandings will leave even the most optimistic dater wondering, "How in the heck am I supposed to meet the right person, and what am I doing wrong?"

I work with hundreds of high-quality, intelligent, attractive, and fascinating people. *Single* people. I am frequently asked, "Marla, if these people are so great, then why are they single? Why do they need to come to a matchmaking service to find someone?" Simple answer, "Because they *are* great people! And truly great people are a rare commodity, and smart enough to get some help finding their perfect other half!" I wrote this follow-up book to help all the readers out there who are equally great single people navigate the dating scene and succeed!

As you read this book, consider me part of your team, coaching you along the way, steering you clear of the pitfalls, and cheering you on. First, we will explore how your attitude, outlook, and energy affect whether or not you are destined to go solo the rest of your life. I don't believe you are, so I will share with you all my inside dating secrets to give you the boost you need to succeed!

I'll tell you the truth about the top desires of both men and women. Wouldn't it be great to know exactly what your date thought of you? Inside I'll share hilarious and brutal feedback from real dates. You might see yourself in some of these common scenarios and finally recognize a pattern that is keeping you from happiness in a long-term relationship. You will definitely get some insight on where and why people are disconnecting, preventing the desired result on both sides!

Come with me and get in the diamond lane on the highway to L-O-V-E!

—Marla

First, Some Background

There is only one happiness in life, to love and be loved.
—George Sand

Matchmaker, Matchmaker, Make Me a Match!

Though pretty much everybody has heard of Match.com or has friends who hooked up on Facebook, the general public knows very little about the modern-day professional matchmaking business and how it works. It's quite a unique profession; I'm the hit of any dinner party. People are fascinated by the details of my job. The two most common questions, which I get asked all the time, are "How did you get into this business?" followed by "How do you match couples? Do you do it all online?"

I love my job and believe that my career was meant to be, but I certainly never aspired to be a matchmaker. I never even had much luck fixing up my friends! I wanted to be an actress and spent most of my time acting or making audition rounds. In the fall of 2001, I was dating the man who would become my husband. He introduced me to a female friend of his, who was taking over a management position at a well-known video dating service called Great Expectations.

Like every working actress, I needed a good part-time gig. She hired me to work in customer relations and also videotape the clients. It was fun. I felt like a movie director, filming the prospective clients and quizzing them on what they were looking for in a mate. Over the next year and a half, I interviewed hundreds of men and women and really perfected my technique, learning as I went how to cut to the heart of what really mattered and also how to present each person in their best light.

After I left Great Expectations due to a management shake-up, I answered a blind ad in the back of an actor's newspaper. The ad was very short, saying only "Talent scout, fun job, Beverly Hills," with a phone number. I decided to check it out since I lived nearby. I called the number and set up an appointment. When I told my friend Fran about my meeting, she tried to talk me out of going. "It's a scam!" she said. "Don't go!" Well, good thing I decided not to listen to her, because when I arrived I found out that the job was recruiting for a matchmaking service called MQI. I was very excited because I had really enjoyed working with singles, helping them try to find the right mate. I was hired on the spot and recruited beautiful single women for the company's male clients, who paid the agency to find them high-quality, marriage-material dates.

Within a couple of months, I was offered a regular position in the office as a matchmaker. I worked four days per week and still went on auditions, but I was enjoying the work so much that I eventually took over the head matchmaking slot and went to work full time. Matchmaking certainly has its challenges (more about that in a moment), but the rewards were enormous. Whenever I learned that a couple I'd introduced had gone "exclusive" or were getting married, I would dance around the office! My work had the potential to change someone's entire life and destiny. I was helping great people find their soul mate—is there anything better than that?

Certainly there were roadblocks along the way. I learned quickly that the two most challenging aspects of matchmaking are clients lying about their age and unrealistic expectations. Both men and women lie shamelessly about their age, and the embarrassing part is that the lie is so obvious. Just the other day a woman came into my office to join our service. She put down on her questionnaire that she was thirty-five years old, when she was clearly not a day under forty-five—if not older! A man told me recently that he was forty-five, when just by looking at him I could easily see he was well into his fifties. I do not feel comfortable lying or even exaggerating to my clients when I match them, so "white lies" about age put me in a very uncomfortable position.

As far as unrealistic expectations go, some clients feel that, because they paid a high fee to a Beverly Hills firm to meet someone, she should be nothing less than a Heidi Klum look-alike, even if he is a Danny DeVito clone.

Another issue comes up when I get a much older man with several kids, seeking only a young woman with no kids. Finding a life partner is not like buying a car, where you can order leather seats, air-conditioning, and a state-of-the-art CD player to your exact specifications. But the reality is, people want what they want, nothing more and nothing less, and I always do my best to deliver.

That's the story, in a nutshell, of how I became a matchmaker. To answer the second-most-common question I hear, no, I do not do my work online at all. I actually hand-match our clients. I don't put them into a computer or let them look through profiles and pick out people that they would like to meet. I sit down with each client and build a "blueprint" of their lifestyle, including what they are looking for in a match, their expectations in love and marriage, and so on. I call the woman first and tell her all about the gentleman I have in mind for her. If she says yes, then I contact the gentleman and give him a good description of her as well as her phone number. I don't show either one photos; they go by my descriptions and trust my instincts.

I've experienced the world of online dating firsthand. When I was single and had just moved from Chicago back to Los Angeles, for a while I carried on a long-distance relationship that eventually wound down. I was fine with not dating at that time, but my aunt and cousin, who were both meeting lots of guys online, talked me into trying it. I went ahead and put up a profile and photo. I didn't have a full-time job yet, which was a good thing because weeding through all of the guys who wrote to me was a daunting task. Nine-tenths didn't even take my requests into consideration.

All they needed to make contact was to like my photo. I wondered if they even bothered to read my profile at all!

I did go ahead and schedule meetings with four of the men who wrote to me. All four were charming in their e-mails and behaved like gentlemen on our dates, but something was not right with each guy. The first one was still technically married, with three kids under the age of five (I had clearly stated that I did not want to meet men with children). The second was an atheist (enough said). The third promised to put me in his movie the minute he met me (yeah, right!), and the fourth was not even the guy in the photo on his profile! He had put up a photo of a model from a magazine instead of his own! Needless to say, that was the end of my Internet dating career. I realized that I personally needed to do some tactical dating to get on track and pinpoint what I was looking for, and not waste my time meeting people who were not even who they claimed to be.

When I set up my clients, the two of them give me feedback after their first date. We've all had dates that we thought went great, but, alas, we never heard from that person again. You can knock your head against the wall and imagine dozens of scenarios, reasons, and excuses, but the fact is you will never know the real answer—unless you have a matchmaker who will give you feedback from your date and give you the answers you seek. They may not be what you want to hear, but I do provide honest answers and real solutions.

This is why I'm such a strong believer in the way I work. The singles I work with are busy in fabulous careers, taking care of family, improving themselves, traveling, and just living life. They don't have time to be out searching for the right person, going to bars, or sitting online for hours as if working a second job. Who has time to waste going on hundreds of coffee dates only to find that each one is a disappointment? Mine has been a very rewarding career. I have introduced countless couples that have gone on to get married, and some have even had children!

It used to be a bit embarrassing to say that you joined a dating service or were online looking for love; now it is so mainstream. Millions of people are outsourcing their dating to a professional! After all, we hire people to clean our house, service our car, make travel arrangements, do business consulting, and so on. Why not hire an expert to weed through the masses and get you closer to finding a perfect partner? These days you'll find countless ads for matchmaking services in magazines and on television, and lately some schools to train matchmakers have even cropped up. Soon I won't have the most unusual job in town anymore!

As the years passed, I realized I had acquired an enormous amount of information about what men and women are really looking for; I'm also an expert on the most common mistakes daters make. I'd been taking notes since my days at Great Expectations, because I knew that this knowledge was entertaining as well as valuable. This book is the culmination of many years and thousands and thousands of dates!

How Did You Meet Your Husband?

"Marla, how did you meet your husband? Was it through your matchmaking service?" I also get asked that question almost every day. Single people, both men and women, are always curious. Many have been searching for their soul mate for years with no results, or have gone through a tough divorce and are having a hard time meeting someone they click with. Quite a few have gone through a string of "bad" relationships and are pretty much fed up with the whole thing. But whatever their situation, they are always curious to know how I got so lucky. Did I have a secret? Well, I *do* kind of have a secret, one that took me years to figure out. It's a formula that I played with throughout the years but never really stuck to. Once I really lived by it, my formula worked like a charm.

It took plenty of trial and error and heartache before I figured out the magic formula. In 1989, I married a man I shouldn't have. He was not ready for marriage and preferred to stay out nights playing poker with the boys rather than come home. He was financially irresponsible, and I was pretty much the last person he wanted to hang out with. I know, bad decision on my part, but I was lonely and he was so cute! Inevitably, we divorced, in 1996.

I moved to Chicago and got myself a little bachelorette pad downtown and a job as a waitress. Suddenly, I was Carrie Bradshaw from *Sex and the City*. Okay, some days I was more like Samantha—well, you get the picture. I should have taken some time for myself but instead jumped right back into trying to find a boyfriend. One positive activity that I did manage to find time for between dates was plenty of reading. I studied metaphysics, went to lectures, and started meditating. That laid some of the groundwork for my later growth.

But for the next five years, I dated constantly, always on the search for "Him." I dated all sorts of guys, hoping that one of them would stick around long enough so that I could at least introduce him as my "boyfriend." I dated a heartless heart surgeon, a Persian lounge singer, a Belgian restaurant manager, a French financial consultant, a Russian mortgage broker, and a slew of others (as you can see, I prefer foreign men!), including a few that I later found out were married or living with their girlfriends. Each time I would get so hopeful and excited, but each time the guy would end up not calling anymore.

Every time a guy dumped me, I would get my hair cut. I think that I wanted to reinvent myself and start fresh. I came to work one day with only about an inch of hair on my head, and a coworker said. "Marla, you'd better stop dating or you're going to be bald soon!"

For a few weeks after each breakup, I would tell myself that was it, no more dating, it wasn't worth it. It led to too much stress and disappointment. But then, of course, another guy would come along and I would tell myself, okay, I'll try it one more time, but that's really it. I'm not the type to ever give up on anything (I've been playing the Lotto for seventeen years), so no matter how disastrous the relationship, I'd always wind up giving dating another go.

In early January 2001, I found out my dad had terminal cancer. He lived in Southern California. So I packed up my apartment and moved to Los Angeles to be with him. Three days after I moved, he died. That same week, the man I had been in a long-distance relationship with for the past four months decided he didn't want a long-distance relationship anymore. He didn't want me to move in with him either, so he broke up with me. Devastated and alone, I stayed with my aunt in Orange County while I looked for an apartment in Hollywood.

In March, I moved into my own place and decided to take some much-needed time for myself. I didn't even find a job right away. My girlfriend Sherry Stipsky invited me one Sunday to go to church with her and three single girl-friends. Services were held at a metaphysical church called Agape International Spiritual Center, and I absolutely loved it. We made attending the weekly service a Sunday ritual. One morning in the car on our way to church, we all made an affirmation that we wanted to find a spiritual man. I gave up concentrating on all of the things I didn't want, and focused on the things that I did. It was at this time my aunt finally convinced me to give Internet dating a try. After those four disappointing dates, I again said to myself, "Enough!" This time I meant it. I started a daily meditation practice and let go of any expectation of finding a man at all.

Maybe I was not meant to be in a relationship. Maybe I would never get married again. I decided that I was totally fine with that and kept up my spiritual practice. I knew two things for sure: I couldn't wait on tables anymore and I couldn't continue the dating game. I totally surrendered my life, in both relationship and career. It felt so good to put the focus on myself for once and not feel the relentless pressure to find "Him."

The way I met the friend who would introduce me to my husband was like a miracle! One night I needed medicine from the drugstore, so I took a walk up Sunset Boulevard to the local Rite-Aid. As I was leaving, I decided to take a look at the vitamins. A little Polish lady and I started chatting. We stood right there in the vitamin section and talked for an hour. We exchanged phone numbers and started seeing each other socially. Sabrina managed an apartment building a few blocks from where I lived, and she enjoyed telling me about the tenants in her building. She kept talking about a guy who lived on the second floor who played piano in a club in Marina Del Rey. She told me all about him: his exercise habits, where he was from, who he was dating. I wondered why she was telling me all of this, and then Sabrina told me that she had checked our astrological charts and that we seemed to be a great match. He did sound intriguing, so I finally said, "Well, maybe I should meet this guy."

She suggested going to see him play at the club. That way I could check him out to see if I was interested. She said she did not tell him we were coming. I found out later that she did tell him, but he was not at all excited. Sabrina had brought girls to the club before to introduce him to but never anyone he found interesting or attractive. Well, I walked right up to the piano, Adolfo stood up, and we both liked what we saw. After he finished work, the three of us returned to Sabrina's apartment for drinks. We sat next to each other on the sofa, our hands touched, and suddenly our lips locked. He likes to say that I kissed him first, but it was like we both had magnets on our lips!

We started seeing each other regularly, and he called me every day. Because of my past experiences, I knew very well that he could stop calling at any time. This time, I remained calm. I was absolutely fine with the situation and left the matter up to the universe. If we were meant to be together, it would work out. I was not even going to think about it. I was finished with stressing myself out wondering if a guy was going to call again or not, and obsessing about what he might be thinking or doing. I continued to focus on my meditation and the things that I wanted. I wanted a spiritual man in my life, I wanted a wonderful relationship, I wanted a man who wanted to be in a relationship, and so on.

A couple of weeks after we met, we were driving in the car and Adolfo looked at me and said, "I asked God to send me someone special." "When did you do that?" I asked. "In December," he said. Wow, I thought, how powerful. It was right after Christmas that my whole life changed and I was brought back to Los Angeles and, seemingly out of the blue, I had met this wonderful man. There were definitely higher forces at work. This was the man for me—not any of those men in Chicago I had tried to force into a relationship. That had been like trying to fit a square peg in a round hole.

A year and a half later, we were married in Mexico City with eighty friends and family members surrounding us. Once I released the situation and didn't try to force anything, everything fell into place, including a new career as a matchmaker helping others to find the love of their life. Whenever we put too much "on" something, whenever we try to force a situation, we actually push it away. It's so tempting to keep on forcing the issue. The desire to find Mr. Right is almost a cultural obsession. We think that we are not complete until we find "the one," when, in fact, we are perfectly complete just as we are. The right man will be a complement to your completeness. Be at peace and all right with yourself, and the rest will show up. Trust me: You don't have to do anything but be okay with where you are right now.

What Is a Soul Mate?

The whole point of dating is to meet your very own soul mate! Since I wrote the book *Excuse Me, Your Soul Mate Is Waiting,* I am often asked the question "What *is* a soul mate?" Is the term overused? Does it really mean anything? I have even had a few people tell me that they don't believe in soul mates. I tend to be partial to the term, because for me it perfectly describes a special connection we have with someone. I find it to be a very powerful term. I believe that soul mates are life partners, close friends, coworkers, pets, or anyone who influences your life in one profound way or another.

We all know the clichés about love at first sight and the feeling that we know someone from a past life. Our perception of a soul mate is often based on movies, television, books, and fairy tales. We love to imagine that magical feeling and experience of finding our soul mate. The problem often arises because romantic love ultimately falls short of that ideal. In romantic love, our feelings are dependent on what we receive in return. We must remember that what we are seeking is unconditional love; more often than not, we not only don't get it, but we don't give it either. A soul mate can challenge us to a higher standard, teach us patience, and lead us to unconditional love.

Finding a soul mate doesn't necessarily mean a forever relationship; a soul mate is here to teach us something and may or may not be with us throughout our lifetime. When the lesson is learned, sometimes we part paths. If we look back on all of the people with whom we have shared loving experiences, it becomes clear that we are not limited to just one soul mate for our lifetime or for eternity. Not all soul mate relationships are meant to be harmonious, and not all soul mate relationships are meant to be long term.

Being with your soul mate does not necessarily mean that you are going to live in bliss, doing everything the same and thinking the same way. Certainly your soul mate can push some of your buttons, and vice versa. I definitely see the need to grow and expand by being with my husband, whom I consider one of my soul mates. I have always tended to have a big mouth and just say whatever I feel, with almost no filter. I really needed to get a handle on that. He challenges me in that area, because his buttons get pushed and he can be quite sensitive in response to my comments, observations, or opinions. I am learning to monitor what I say, which is a good thing since I tend to talk too much and too freely. Living with him is good training for me, unbeknownst to him, in being more selective with my comments in general. While we are very happy being with each other and would not want to be apart, we also drive each other crazy on occasion with our personality flaws that need some attention.

Soul mates aren't necessarily always other humans! Another soul mate for me is my dog Daphne. She made her transition in April 2007 after almost seventeen years with me. We were so close and communicated on a very deep level with such absolute unconditional love that I was transformed by her presence. We still have a deep connection even though she is not here in the physical sense. I absolutely believe that a pet can be a soul mate.

I'll bet you have friends with whom you connected from the word hello and your relationship developed into a very close and meaningful one. This sense of immediate connection arises from unconscious or soul memories of previous loving experiences. The metaphysical definition of a soul mate is someone you knew in a past life. A soul mate, then, is someone with whom we have shared many past life experiences. Most soul mates are predestined before you were born. Soul mates are our soul family, the ones we have for many lifetimes, and our experiences with them help us grow and create and dissipate karma. A soul mate is someone you are close to at a soul level, and with whom you have had many shared experiences in different lifetimes, in various kinds of relationships.

Soul mates can create happy marriages as they are working on similar life lessons and projects in this lifetime. Since they have been friends over many lifetimes, they might need each other to complete their work or mission. Soul mates can also experience a stable connection like a brother-sister type of rapport as opposed to a romantic relationship.

Twin Flames

I only recently learned about twin flames. I find it a fascinating subject. The term is often confused with that of soul mates, though the two are different. A twin flame reunion is the most fulfilling relationship we can have. It is more intense than any other union. Twin flame couples are extremely rare, because a twin flame is literally the other half of our soul.

In the beginning, when we were created by God in an ovoid white-fire-spirit-light, the soul was split like the atom into two identical parts, each with the same identical soul blueprint. After being split, the two souls went their separate ways, incarnating over and over, gathering human experiences before coming back together. When twins get together, it is for some kind of spiritual work. When twin flames reunite, they experience an acceleration of their spiritual growth and awakening.

Karmic Relationships

Karmic relationships are those in which the other person owes you a karmic debt or you owe them from a former life. The relationship will often end when the debt is paid—remember, all relationships are for mutual personal evolution. You may be in a karmic relationship if you feel drained physically, emotionally, or financially by another.

So, now it is time to meet your soul mate! No need to worry or try to analyze whether or not the person you meet is your soul mate, twin flame, or someone who owes you a karmic debt! Just concentrate on honing your dating skills, being the best you, and feeling great, so that you can meet the man you want to spend the rest of your life with: your very own definition of your "soul mate"!

Living Your Truth to Be Your Best You!

How many cares one loses when one decides not to be something but to be someone.

—Coco Chanel

The Way We Were

As I write these words, I am sitting at the busy Starbucks on Rush Street in downtown Chicago, my old neighborhood hangout. I am in town for a week to promote my first book, *Excuse Me, Your Soul Mate Is Waiting.* I am sitting in the same exact spot where I once spent hours with an old boyfriend. Hanging out, drinking our lattes, we were in love and enjoying every moment together. I expected that relationship to last. When we broke up shortly thereafter, I was crushed. I returned to Starbucks and sat by myself at the same table to recreate that wonderful feeling, but I ended up choking back the tears.

Now, sitting in this chair remembering that time, I cannot believe that eight years have passed. The Starbucks looks exactly the same—I wish I could say that about myself! But there have been big changes within me. I am no longer that insecure, desperate-to-be-with-a-guy girl, wasting valuable time on unavailable men. It feels great to look back and realize how much I have learned and grown in all areas of my life, not only in romantic relationships, but in my career and friendships as well. With lots of reading, workshops, meditation, praying, self-reflection, and just plain maturity I have finally come to a place where I feel calmer and in control—feeling good about where I am and what I'm doing! I still have much more to achieve and learn and there's always room to grow, but the difference is remarkable. When we make a commitment to never stop expanding and bettering ourselves, all areas of our lives start to sparkle.

Sometimes in order to call in new and wonderful experiences and up the level of our lives to a higher vibrational frequency, we need to let go of some old habits, friends, or situations. To make room in your heart and life for a wonderful romantic partner, take stock of what negative or lower energies are inhabiting your space and cluttering up your life. In the past six or seven years, some old friends who were not growing, expanding, and making the commitment to live at the level I sought gradually fell out of my life. I had to tell one old friend I would not be making contact again. I still hold these people in high regard, remember them fondly, and wish them well, but they no longer fit into the way I am living my life.

Friends, acquaintances, jobs, and possessions all come into our lives for a reason. Some stay for a season; others for a lifetime. They are not all meant to stay with us forever! In my case, I know that my past romantic relationships, although temporary, taught me invaluable lessons that I needed in order to grow. My partners probably needed to learn something from me as well. If you don't take stock and take a good hard look at what qualities are important to you in your friends and your romantic relationships, then you will end up with the same people in your life over and over again—just wearing different clothes.

The universe is made of energy, and human beings are also made of energy. We want to vibrate at a high frequency and stay in a positive mode the majority of the time. When you do this, you will begin to attract the right people and situations into your life, those who are most beneficial to your well-being and growth.

Take Some Time for Spiritual Growth

As adults we are often so busy trying to be in control and make everything happen that we forget to breathe and let spirit in. Taking the time to sit quietly by yourself and contemplate what you would like to attract and create in your life is so important in the hectic world in which we live. The images in our mind create what is happening to us—good and bad—all the time. Learn to tune in and listen to your inner guidance, trust your heart, and be gentle with yourself. As you continue to expand and grow in your spiritual work and awareness, you will notice that the world around you has also started to expand and grow in a much more positive way.

Live Your Truth

When you are living your truth with integrity, you will soon notice how everything in your life seems to just fall in place, as if it were meant to be. Maybe not all at once, but as you continue to work and stretch, you will realize slowly but surely that invisible forces are aligning with you and helping you reach your goals. This is living your life *with purpose* and *on purpose*.

When I was a little girl, I loved to read and also liked to write poetry. I turned out hundreds of poems; they just flowed out of me. I remember sitting in the living room at my Grandma Martenson's house when I was about eight years old, reading her some of my latest work. She would say with awe, "My Marla can write a poem just like that!" as she snapped her fingers.

I also carried around a sketchpad and some charcoal and used to sketch everything I saw, including portraits of her. I wasn't too good, but it was fun. My grandma had a piano, and I used to sit on the bench for hours "playing" and "singing" songs that I pretended to read from the pages of music she had stored in the piano bench. At family gatherings I used to tap dance for everyone. I put on variety shows for the neighborhood; I practiced TV commercials in the bathroom mirror; I took ballet, tap, jazz, piano, cello, singing, baton, and acting classes. I was driven to create and perform, and God bless my parents for going along with it all.

I dreamed my way through junior high, picturing myself as a movie star. My grandma wholeheartedly believed in my talents and used to say, "Hold your head up high—when you've got it, flaunt it!" She was an Elizabeth Taylor type, dark hair and blue eyes, the most glamorous grandma around. She was a bit heavyset, but I thought she was fabulous! She had a full-time job and she liked to drive fast. She always wore full makeup and jewelry and her signature perfume, Emeraude by Coty. I know that I inherited my dramatic flair from her. After she died, I found a bottle of her perfume in the linen closet. I used to go and smell it to remind me of her.

I was clearly destined to be in a creative field. I was hopeless at math, science, and history, but got good marks in English, reading, drama, and languages. At the age of three, I was pretending to speak Spanish. (How ironic that I am married to a man from Mexico, and now I do speak Spanish—on a daily basis!) Even though I studied singing and musical instruments diligently, I was noticeably lacking in musical talent. I also tried to draw and paint—also hopeless. I *was* a good dancer, actress, and writer.

I moved to Hollywood at the age of twenty to pursue an acting career. I did some TV commercials and print modeling but always had to work in the restaurant business to pay my bills. From the start, I knew that I did not belong in *that* business. I had more to offer than seating people, bringing them their club sandwich, or clearing their dirty dishes. Unfortunately, at that age I was more concerned with the men in my life and meeting more of them than my career or my own well-being. If I'd put half the energy into my career that I spent pursuing these various Mr. Wrongs, I'd have won an Academy Award! The result of these misplaced priorities was that I did not succeed as an actress. I eventually let that dream go, but the nagging feeling in the back of my mind that I should write never left me. I didn't share that desire with anyone, but the idea was always there in the background, haunting me.

When I finally put the acting and meaningless restaurant jobs firmly on the side to make a real living at the age of thirty-nine, I got into matchmaking. I also turned to writing again—after thirty-five years. I would never have dreamed that at the age of forty-five I would become a published author! It blew me away when I actually sat down and thought about it. My original desire, interest, calling, pull—whatever you want to call it—was the exact thing that I was meant to do! I felt more happy and alive than I ever had when I was sitting at my computer creating books to inspire others.

The point to this story is that once I refused to go back to the restaurant business and began to live my truth, everything fell into place. My soul mate arrived to love, help, and support me; the right friends and contacts magically appeared to facilitate my writing career; and I finally felt that I was giving something, instead of always trying to get. I am so proud to have introduced countless couples that have gone on to get married. I am thrilled to have written a book that has offered hope and helped people to find their own soul mate. And I am most proud that I have finally found my calling and am living my truth, even if it is at age forty-five. I might be having hot flashes, but they're nothing compared to the fire in my soul that comes from finally living my dream and sharing it with my soul mate!

Dating Assignment

Write down five things that you can do to start living your truth.

1._____

2._____

3._____

4._____

5._____

Be an Original: How Self-Esteem Plays an Important Role in Dating

I recently received this e-mail from one of my readers:

> My name is Terri, I am twenty-five years old, and I have problems with dating and with myself. When I was in high school, I was the reserved and shy type of person and I am still this way in the present. I think that the reason for this was my family telling me how I wasn't smart enough, that I had poor comprehension, and that I had no talent. And my peers in school were no better. I have been told things and heard how something was wrong with me because I'm not like everyone else. I wasn't in a rush to get a boyfriend or have sex. I did have a guy who showed interest, like a guy in the band. I still have guys who are interested in me, but when it comes to being in a relationship and being committed, I feel like I have nothing to give at this point because I don't have the experience. I have never really had a boyfriend but I casually date. I feel like I'm not good enough. I feel like I will be rejected. Can you please help me in any way, shape, or form?

This girl obviously has self-esteem issues, which lie at the heart of her trouble with romantic relationships. Sadly, many of us have heard the same negative things that Terri heard growing up, leading directly to difficulty with relationships as an adult.

What exactly does it mean to have high self-esteem? Self-esteem is simply how a person perceives him or herself.

Good self-esteem means that we see a positive meaning to our place in the world as well as believe that we have a true purpose in life. Unfortunately, a lot of us let other people's opinions and comments affect our belief that we have an important and valuable role to play and contributions to make in this life. These remarks rule the way we conduct ourselves and hinder us from living our truth. Oftentimes our parents, peers, and others who make these judgments have no idea of the damage they are doing.

Growing up, I was very bad at math, science, and history. I was a creative person. My parents would shrug and say, "Oh, well, Marla just isn't good in school." There was no incentive for me to even try to get good grades. If I came home with Ds or Fs on my report card, the feeling was just, "Oh, well, that's just Marla, she's no brainiac!" I wound up marrying, at the age of twenty-seven, a man who told me constantly for seven years how stupid I was.

I *was* smart enough to realize that the reason he constantly belittled my intelligence was because he himself felt "less than." He had started as a teen working full time and became an incredibly talented chef, but never developed his intellectual side. His spelling, for example, was at about a second-grade level. He was keenly aware of his shortcomings, but of course refused to admit them, preferring instead to take his feelings out on me by tearing down my self-esteem.

Even if you are aware of the reasons that people are making careless and hurtful comments about you, their words can permeate your psyche and negatively affect your decisions in every area of your life. This man was not the only person who told me how dumb I was over the years. It not only hurt, but it was also very frustrating and exhausting work trying to convince them otherwise. I had to do so much spiritual work to counteract their negativity that I sometimes wondered how I could manage to keep my vibration high and not believe the lies I was hearing about myself over and over again.

Anytime someone tells you that you are "less than" in any area, know that the issue is completely theirs, because ultimately everything that people say and do is *all about them*. Realize that you are a special, unique individual with your own talents and strengths and are not required to prove yourself to anyone. You *are* good enough to have a boyfriend, the career you choose, and the life you desire! Don't look to the world for your validation; everything that you need is within you!

Terri mentions in her e-mail that she was told that something was wrong with her because she's not like everyone else. For one thing, everyone is different. There is no way to be "like everyone else." Even if you could, how boring would that be? I just love being an original. There is no one in the world like me—or you! Everyone should celebrate and value how truly unique they are!

A great exercise for raising your self-esteem is to write down five wonderful qualities you possess and five things at which you excel. We all have unique qualities and talents. Even if you believe there is absolutely nothing special about you, believe me, there is. Think back to what others have said about you, if you have to. What compliments have you received in your life? You've probably never forgotten some of them. Take this opportunity to remember them, write them down, and reflect on just how special you truly are.

Dating Exercise

List five traits that make you uniquely wonderful!

1._____

2._____

3._____

4._____

5._____

List five areas in which you excel.

1._____

2._____

3._____

4._____

5._____

List five accomplishments of which you are proud.

1._____

2._____

3._____

4._____

5._____

Embrace Your Alone Time!

Knowing and being happy that no one else is quite like you should be a fabulous feeling! When you are able to wholeheartedly acknowledge and celebrate your special talents, abilities, and accomplishments, you are well on your way to solid self-esteem—and being a good date!

The goal of this book is to help readers be the best dater they can be—but remember, *there is nothing wrong with being alone*. It is easy to fall into the trap of thinking that you must be in a relationship every minute, but actually being on your own for a while is extremely beneficial. Both being single and being in a relationship have their positive and negative points. Don't forget: When you live with someone, you have to compromise on many things. You can no longer decorate exactly the way you want to. You may have to deal with someone snoring, or tossing and turning and keeping you awake every night. You have to let someone know when you are coming home and be accountable in almost every way. And that's just the small stuff.

So learn to live large while you are single! Use this time to do your inner work, read, better yourself, take classes, get in shape, volunteer, learn a new language, anything that will improve your self-esteem, further your goals, get you closer to your own truth, and make you an even more interesting person when you do meet someone! Take this valuable time to evaluate yourself while waiting for Prince Charming to arrive: Can you honestly say that you are living your best life? Are you working in a job that you love? Is the work you do making a difference in the world or at least to somebody? Are you spending quality time with loved ones, making time for contemplation and prayer, living in the now, savoring each moment?

Whether a romantic love partner comes into your life or not, you can choose to express love every day in so many ways. You can offer a smile to a stranger, a hug to a friend, or time to play with a child. You could lend a sympathetic ear to someone with a problem, write a check to a charity, mail a card to a friend to brighten her day, or do any one of a hundred things that will bring some cheer to another. Your life becomes so much richer and more rewarding when you focus on giving rather than getting.

I can attest to the truth of that concept. All of the years that I was pursuing an acting career, I was always trying to "get." I was either trying to get an audition, get in to see a casting director, get money to take a certain class, or just get some attention; my whole life was spent just trying to get! Even though that's the name of the game when you pursue a career like acting—you've got to shmooze, get out there, meet people, and get something going—my destiny was always in someone else's hands. I was continually reaching for something that was just a bit out of my reach. I did get some work, but it was never enough to pay the bills.

When I went into a field in which I was helping people (matchmaking), the focus shifted from trying to get to giving, helping, and being of service. That led to me being blessed to be able to write a book that has helped even more people! Everything in my life flows much more easily and naturally now. In the process of giving, I am getting more than I could have hoped for.

Dating Exercise

List five new things that you can do to live your life to the fullest today.

1._____

2._____

3._____

4._____

5._____

List three things that you can give instead of trying to get.

1._____

2._____

3._____

Clear Out the Clutter!

When our homes become cluttered, other aspects of our lives tend to feel gridlocked too. Clutter is both a symptom and a cause of stuck energy. I know in my own life, when my desk is a mess, I can't write as freely, and when my bedroom where I keep all of my books, magazines, and a lot of other stuff is cluttered, I feel like I am suffocating.

Clutter takes many forms: old Christmas or birthday cards, mugs or shot glasses that you brought home from vacation but never use, junk mail that piles up, old books or magazines that you will never read again. Remember: Everything that surrounds you should be working for you in some way.

If you are hoping to manifest a soul mate and a wonderful life with him, then you must take a good hard look at your living space and make sure that the energy is flowing, not clogged! If you met him tomorrow, would there even be space for your dream man to move in? If you move in with him or get a new place together, how much unnecessary stuff will you be dragging along with you?

Clearing clutter creates space for us to discover our true path in life, who we want to become, and what experiences we want to create. Just as clutter keeps energy stagnant, it can also keep other areas of your life from growing (not to mention that material clutter leads to mental clutter and stress, which can eventually develop into stress-related illnesses and chronic disease). Clearing out the old ensures that there is space for the new. When you clear your clutter, you take a concrete step toward regaining your power, and you create space for wonderful new things and relationships to come into your life.

THREE

Age: Why It Matters

*A woman's unhappiness is to rely on her youth. Youth must
be replaced with mystery.*

—Coco Chanel

Unless You Make a Deal with
the Devil, You Are Going to Age!

Though it was once not considered "polite" to ask
someone his or her age (especially a woman), people are
now more likely than not to blurt out, "How old are you?"
Worse, if they don't believe your answer, they'll ask again,
"No, how old are you really?" Age is referenced all the time.
"Nicole Kidman, 41, was seen out with John Doe, 42, who
recently ended a romantic relationship with Molly Dolly,
34, who is now dating Joe Schmo, 29."

Why are we all so obsessed with age? When I was

thirty-five and living in Chicago, I told a guy I worked with my age. I will never forget his reaction! Sounding both surprised and mortified, the guy said to me, "Oh, my God, you're *that* old? I never would have guessed!" Then, perhaps trying to wedge his foot out of his mouth, he added, "You look really good for thirty-five." My coworker may have thought he was giving me a compliment, but I took it to mean that, being *that* old, I should already be a wreck, but somehow by the grace of God (or freak of nature), I was still holding up. "Yes," I said, "I'm thirty-five. Luckily, I can still manage to dress myself and get around without a walker! Amazing, isn't it?"

Another time, a man I was dating told me I was "well preserved." I felt like a piece of antique furniture! In my business, I constantly hear the phrase, "She looks really good for her age" or "He looks so young for his age." I don't understand why anyone has to "look good for his/her age." In my opinion, someone either looks good or they don't—their actual age is irrelevant! Some of us have taken extremely good care of ourselves over the years and it shows, while others may have smoked all the time, caught too many rays, and had a few too many cocktails along the way, among other things. As people age, all that damage shows. Maybe I'm way off, but I never feel complimented when someone tells me that I look good for my age. I just feel that they are saying that I am old, but don't look *that* old yet, like I should. I would rather be told nothing at all. (My husband thinks I'm a ten, with or without my Botox! And that's all that matters!)

Most people seem to have a definite idea about what a certain age "looks like." Age (even for those under twenty, who think that everyone older than twenty-five is "ancient") is a baseline from which all other things about that person are measured. Consider these comments:

"You look good (for your age)."

"You've accomplished so much (for someone your age)."

"You're very mature (for your age)."

"I admire that you're still so ambitious (for someone your age)."

"You're not financially secure (at your age)?"

"You're having a baby (at your age)?"

"You're in pretty good shape (for someone your age)."

Of course, physical "preservation" is often equated with age, as is sexual prowess, but consider this interesting take on it. When one of my girlfriends told a guy she was forty, he said, "You're forty? You don't *walk* like you're forty." Say what? Yes, people seem to have definite ideas about age, and you can bet that when men and women are looking for a partner, age is an important part of the equation (even if they say it is not!).

Which brings me to the issue of lying about your age in the dating arena. As I mentioned earlier, this is one of the most challenging aspects of my job. Every day I have the advantage of seeing and hearing about what is really going on out there, and here is my take on this touchy subject.

I Might Be "Old," but I Still Feel Young

You might look young and feel young, but lying about your age almost always comes back to bite you. Even though it might get you to second base with someone, when they find out about your dishonesty and your actual age, you'll rarely get to third base, or especially "home." Sustaining a lie over a period of time can slow down the process of weeding out the "no-gos" so you're not free to get on with finding the person who is "perfect" for you. This is not to say that lying isn't tempting. In an age when being injected with Botox can have higher payoffs than being infused with character, you can be sure that fibbing about one's age is happening a lot!

Greta is a "young" forty-five, but she feels she must lie about her age to increase her chances of getting her "ideal" date. She tells me, "Who is going to want to date a woman older than thirty-five? I don't want to get stuck just dating the old guys, but if I lay my age on the line right off the bat, my chances for dating guys my own age are over." Luckily for Greta and other women like her, at a time when fifty is the new forty, and forty is the new thirty, we can often get away with telling a guy to his face that we are younger, and they may well believe it. But does this dating tactic work? Not too often.

As a professional matchmaker, it has been my experience that women want me to put a *younger* age down on their file, saying that they'll "come clean" about their real age at a later date. Their reasoning is that if potential matches know the truth about their age, they won't want to meet them, but if they get a chance to see them in person, they'll be so impressed by the "total package," as well as their youthful appearance, that age will no longer matter. (And yes, men lie about their age too, and for the same reasons.) But lying is not a good idea. Keep in mind that when it comes to finding a "partner for life," you're not auditioning for a part in a movie. You are looking to meet your life partner, and traits like truth and integrity matter! It's not smart to start off a relationship with even a "little white lie."

Yes, I know that many of us do not look, act, or feel our age, but even if we feel we are "ageless and timeless," honesty really is the best policy when it comes to "interviewing" someone if you're looking to become "Mr. & Mrs." Besides, once you're a couple, you can't keep your driver's license or your passport under the mattress forever!

Age Matters—Here's Why

Whether you're looking to experience something for the first time, or you've been there, done that, age is a milestone of sorts, representing experiences that become significant and important to our hopes and dreams in life. Here are some reasons why age matters when looking for "the right one."

Age and Energy Level: A certain age category is often equated with stamina and, in particular, energy. Although men are often more "adamant" about the importance of a woman's age, the same "age-is-important" mentality is true for women too. Regardless of their age, the majority of men invariably say they are not all that interested in dating "older women" (which men define as age forty-plus) even if they are attractive, bright, and sexy because "they have no energy and can't keep up with me." Many men say that once a woman hits her late forties, her energy level drops significantly and she no longer wants to do many of the things he's interested in doing. Try as you might to convince a man that energy does not seep out of a woman's body as though it were a punctured balloon once she reaches the big four-O, most just don't buy it.

We can all cite examples of fifty-year-old women friends who run major corporations and, in their spare time, ride horses, go whitewater rafting, hike, bike, play tennis and golf, and more! My own aunt Cheryl just turned sixty-two, and she typically works twelve-hour days and goes out in the evenings with her fabulous fiancé Ed (whom she met in her late fifties). On the weekends she plays in tennis matches, hikes, plays some golf, cleans the house, runs errands, and looks fabulous doing it all wearing a size four! So ladies, I do know that men can be out of touch on this issue.

Recently, I told a man in my dating service that he really must meet a remarkable woman who, while ten years younger than him, was still five years older than the age limit he specified was "right" for him. After I talked about how lovely she was and listed all of her interests, activities, and wonderful accomplishments (which made the two of them extremely compatible), it was only after much persuasion on my part that he "gave in" and agreed to meet her. The good news is that he called a week later and confessed how active, in shape, and fabulous this lady was!

Months have passed, and they are still seeing each other. Alas, this couple is the exception to the rule.

Women, though less vocal about a man's age, and yes, a little less biased and more flexible in letting age be a make-or-break factor, also say that age matters as it relates to energy level. If a thirty-year-old says she's looking for someone in his eighties, well, she's most likely not looking for someone who enjoys her passion for skiing, or at least not accompanying her on black diamond ski trails. If she is sixty, she may not be looking for someone in his thirties or forties unless she is simply admitting she doesn't mind being with a man who's merely looking for a "sponsor" and not a love match.

There are plenty of women who would agree with Kim Cattrall's recent remark, "I think dating a younger man is great because they have great energy, and are easily intimidated, and that's always a good thing." That comment says a lot, don't you think? I also adore the comment by Ivana Trump, "I cannot be with an older man. They are too set in their ways. I prefer to be a baby-sitter than a nursemaid."

Age and the "Soon I'll Look Like My Mother" Fear: Jeanne had just started seeing Michael, who was really smitten when he first met her. On each date, he confirmed how "refreshing" it was to find a "woman like her." Certainly, he had many complaints about his previous attempts to find love. Though now living in California, he was originally from the Midwest and said that dating in "Flake-land" (California) was tough and he "wanted nothing to do with the girls here." When he learned about Jeanne, who was also residing in California and originally from the Midwest, he was more than willing to meet "a girl with Midwest values."

Michael liked everything about Jeanne: "the way she dresses, the way she smells, her work ethic, her consideration and kindness, her beauty, inside and out." But Jeanne's positive attributes and Midwest values suddenly became less appealing to Michael once he learned her age. Although he was three years older than Jeanne, when she revealed her age on their tenth date, he was genuinely disappointed because he thought she was ten years younger!

Why was Michael so disappointed that she was not as young as he had guessed her to be? Because Michael, like many men, say they fear that once women reach age forty, "they'll get old and fat and look like my (or her) mother." When Jeanne saw the look of disappointment in Michael's eyes when she told him her age, he leveled with her, saying, "I just want to be married to a really pretty woman, someone who is going to be pretty for a long, long time."

To this, Jeanne, ever the spitfire, replied, "Well, I want to be married to a really together guy, and taking *your* age into consideration, I'll probably outlive you by twenty years, so actually, I'll most likely have the chance to be a pretty woman for at least two men in my lifetime!" Despite their "age issues," Jeanne and Michael are still going out. I'll keep you posted . . . .

I remember as a child, my brother, who was about ten years old at the time, had a crush on a little girl who lived up the street. One day he went to her house for lunch. When he came home, he announced that he was no longer interested in her because her mother had a big butt. He fig-ured if the mom had a big butt, the daughter eventually would too. My mom and I had a good laugh. Thank good-ness our own mother had a great figure, so no guys ever judged me on my mother's girth. Apparently, men form these ideas about women and their mothers in childhood. Very interesting, isn't it?

But seriously, do women get "old and fat" after forty? Many do. But many women today do not. And for the sin-gle gals who intend to find Mr. Right, many do not intend to lose him because she stops being attractive to him. As my girlfriend Elisabeth told me, "I intend to look good for the guy in my life because I know the importance of 'eye candy' in making sure that all his more interesting body parts work!" What do I have to say to that? "Smart girl, lucky guy!"

You see, Elisabeth has figured out one vital truth behind men's fear of "old women." It's easier to stay sexu-ally active when the woman is fit and attractive. I hate to have to state this truth so bluntly, but that's just the way it is! Of course, it's all right for him (in his estimation) to look worse than homeless on Saturday morning when he declares he doesn't intend to shave for the weekend and why should he toss those twenty-year-old running shorts? Well, that's why God created chocolate—to help women cope with such frustrations! (Luckily, there is also couple's counseling.)

Bottom line: Looks, and therefore age, are important factors in a man's desire to pursue you. (Yes, yes, we know that for approximately two percent of the male population that is not true.) But if you are dating someone in the other ninety-eight percentile, it's important to understand the basics of the "romance gene" for the male gender and what it takes to attract his interest in romancing you. And they say women are complicated!

Age and the Biological Clock: That ticking clock can affect both men and women. If you're a woman who still wants children, you may not want to marry a much older man who won't be around to raise a family or has no desire to start one in the first place. And yes, there are men in their late forties and fifties who still want to have children of their own. But these men tend to gravitate to women who are much younger. By the time they date an older woman long enough to really know each other, and then have a year or two alone together after marrying, it may be too late to start a family. So a man generally won't take a chance on a forty-something woman if he still wants children. If he doesn't mind adopting or helping her raise her own children, that's another matter.

Of course, a woman does not want to be with a man who wants to start a family if she doesn't want that too. Nor should she ever be less than honest about wanting to have a baby if she's still childless but hoping. So whatever your needs and wants are in terms of having children—whether it be having your own children or finding a partner who already has their own—age will come into play.

Age and Youth: Age definitely matters for men who simply want to date young things, "just because." And, yes, women sometimes want to date "younger" too, but this is usually the exception to the rule. Brad is a good example of someone who will only date younger women. Although Brad is sixty-five and more suited for dating someone in her early fifties, he won't even consider dating a woman in her late forties. In fact, ideally, he would like only to date women who are thirty-something, and actually prefers twenty-somethings. He certainly wouldn't pass up an eighteen-year-old if he could get her to say yes to a date. He especially fawns over models and famous young tennis players (which says it all!).

Even though Brad is sixty-five and *looks* sixty-five, he thinks he looks young. Like most men who think the way Brad does, they say young women are "fresh-looking and more fun to be with, and they aren't bitter with as much baggage as older women." (I've heard that reasoning so many times, my head could explode!) It is probably no surprise that Brad admits he is lonely. And, not surprisingly, the women or "girls" he is interested in are not interested in him.

Age and Experience: Age also matters when it comes to "experience." It takes plenty of living to put experiences under your belt. Women tend to love it when a man has done something significant in life; achievement represents a good work ethic and is equated with "being successful" or at least a good provider. Some men also like and respect being with a woman who has many achievements and has been around the world a bit. But, let's face it, to most men, a partner's realm of achievement is less important than it is to a woman. Many men would prefer to date someone younger rather than a woman with an impressive resume of achievements. This is especially true for men who have had mostly traditional marriages where the wife stayed home and cared for a family.

Women, on the other hand, may not be looking for a man with a fifteen-page resume, but very few women ask to see men more than ten years younger than they are—because these men really haven't had time to "make something of themselves" yet. Women really do prefer men with whom they have something in common, and many times those commonalities come down to having raised a family, valuing family and friends, and the basic core values of safety, comfort, and willingness to be in a mutually loving relationship. Much of this is a function of "time under one's belt"—in other words, years of living and learning lessons. Mature men, of course, share these values as well. The good news is that age can be a common denominator in looking for mature and committed love.

Age and What Other People Think: Oftentimes, a gal will decline to meet a gentleman who happens to be quite a few years older than she is because "he's almost as old as my dad!" Many women cannot imagine themselves being with someone from their parents' generation. Even if they could possibly have much in common, some women are concerned about getting involved with someone significantly older, as it may appear to others that he's a "sugar daddy."

Very few men, however, worry that dating a much younger woman will arouse looks of scorn. In fact, most will happily and proudly date a younger woman because it is a boost to their ego, as if they want to proclaim, "I'm potent and virile—as you can see by the young 'eye candy' on my arm." Never mind that most of the time after she gets dropped off, she calls one of the young guys she's seeing and invites him over. Yes, she's available to go out with her senior citizen if he's got great tickets to the best events in town. This same man who loves to show her off, of course, would rarely consider dating a woman his own age.

Age and Financial Security: We'd all be kidding ourselves if we said that financial security wasn't important to us. How many of us have married not for love as much for financial security (or selected one man over another because we thought he had a more "secure" future)? Yes, there are gold diggers among us. Anna Nicole Smith's wedding to a man in his nineties prompted comedienne Roseanne Barr to say on national television, "Did you hear about Anna Nicole Smith marrying that old millionaire guy in his nineties? I just want to know if he has an older brother!" Women are more likely to equate age with security; the more years under his belt, the more time he's had to make and invest money. What Anna Nicole Smith did sounds like a pretty good idea to a certain group of women, who say, "I'd rather be an old man's sweetheart than a young man's gofer." For a woman who says she's looking for a much older guy, her agenda is usually to be taken care of.

Not that this is a deterrent to many senior gentlemen! Some of these "great-granddaddies" will accept the fact that a woman is after his cash because he's willing to trade it for companionship with a "pretty young thing." But financial concerns aren't merely important to women; men too take money into consideration. When a man has money, he usually doesn't mind marrying someone who has none, but if a man has no money, he definitely prefers someone who will at least give him a hand in bringing in an income. Although some men find it demeaning to be dependent on a woman financially, most are happy to find someone to help share the load. And, yes, there is no shortage of gigolos!

We Are Always the "Perfect Age" for Someone

Age—for all the reasons given, it matters! There are sound concerns and shallow ones, which may not seem fair, but age is a reality a dater must be prepared to contend with. Consider these numbers: There are eighty-six million single adults in the United States. If you are between the ages of twenty-five and twenty-nine, you have nine million unattached peers. If you're between the ages of thirty-five and forty-four, you singles are thirteen million strong. And if you're fifty-five to sixty-four, you have 2.3 million single contemporaries. As these numbers show, there are enough singles for all of us!

Given that there is so much competition out there, we are all beginning to take better care of ourselves. Our perceptions of what we can and cannot do are changing as well. More "older" women are out there hiking, biking, getting their black belts in karate, spinning, boxing, and mountain climbing. And more "older" men are not afraid to be fit and, yes, even sensitive!

I urge my clients and readers to keep an open mind: Try not to judge a person by a number—you might be pleasantly surprised! Each age has its own special joys and experiences, so capitalize on those. We are always the perfect age for where we are in life, most especially if we truly want to find a partner.

Age does not protect you from love, but love to some extent protects you from age.

—Jeanne Moreau

Dating Quiz

Taking Stock: Here is your chance to see how important age is to you in deciding whether you're willing to commit to someone.

• Do you have a specific age range in mind for someone you'd like to be with? If so, what is it?

• Why do you believe this age range is "good" for you?

• List three ways you've experienced a date's age as significant in terms of that person being someone you would marry:

1. _____

2. _____

3. _____

• Have you ever been attracted to someone much older because he appeared to be financially successful?

• Have you ever been attracted to someone much younger because you enjoyed the looks and admiration that being with this person garnered from others?

- Have you ever rejected an older date because you feared that he wouldn't be able to "keep up" with you, or that his physical appearance might soon deteriorate?

- Are you attracted to people who have done a lot of interesting things in life, who have a lot of experiences under their belt?

- Have you ever lied about your age or avoided telling it to a potential or current date? If yes, why?

- If you found out later that a date lied about his age, but you really liked the person, would you continue to see him?

If you answered these questions honestly, I bet you said yes to at least one of them. That's okay—it's a reality in today's world, because age does matter. Therefore it's important to analyze your feelings and preferences regarding age *before* entering into a dating relationship. Why spend time with someone whose age will most likely become an "issue" between you? On the other hand, if your age criterion is too strict, you might want to broaden your mind and expand that age range a bit. Age tends to be one of those make-or-break issues for most couples. Make sure you know what ages work for you, and you'll find yourself making smarter dating decisions.

FOUR

What Do Men Want?

Sometimes I wonder if men and women really suit each other. Perhaps they should live next door and just visit now and then.

—Katharine Hepburn

Does He Just Want an Arm Piece?

I am convinced that deep down everyone hopes to find his or her true love. This may not seem true when you go on date after date, year after year, and nothing ever seems to come of the process. The company I work for is specialized; we match financially upscale professional men with beautiful women. Naturally, some women in our service wonder if these guys are serious or just looking for a good time. One of the questions I hear most often from the women at my job is "Are these men really serious about finding someone, or do they just want an arm piece?"

Since men are visual creatures, it only makes sense that when plunking down thousands of dollars for a matchmaking service, they choose the one that offers good-looking, slender women. It's similar to offering women the choice of meeting successful men, rather than men who are flat broke and struggling. Still, I meet women who have a hard time accepting the fact that their looks are the first thing a man is interested in. But no man is going to approach a woman he does not find attractive and say, "Hi, my name is Jim, you look like you have a beautiful soul and a brilliant mind, would you like to have dinner sometime?"

Men are hardwired to respond to visual cues, and there is nothing that any of us can do about that. To become aroused and have his "apparatus" work, he needs to like what he sees! Most men will not become excited looking at flab and cellulite. Why do you think that celebrity males pair up with the hottest women in Hollywood and not some nice, plump plain Jane? It's the same reason that advertising agencies hire gorgeous models to sell everything from cars to hamburgers.

My husband is sitting next to me as I am writing this, watching television, and I just glanced up to see a smoking-hot woman in low-rise jeans riding a mechanical bull and eating a hamburger to the rock-and-roll song *Slow Ride*. Now, few of us are blessed with the gene pool of, say, Cameron Diaz, Heidi Klum, or Eva Longoria, but we can still get our behinds to the gym or walk around the block a few times per day and cut out the junk food.

The way we look greatly affects our ability to attract and keep a partner. A man knows if he is physically interested in a woman within the first three minutes of meeting her. For men, attraction occurs on a biological level; he wants to know that he can successfully pass on his genes, which is why men are generally attracted to younger women. For women, the man that is most attractive to her tends to be the one who can provide food, shelter, and care for a family, which is why women are often attracted to older men. In the dating game, *staying slim and trim is probably the most important thing you can do to ensure that you will attract a man and then keep him interested once you do.*

More vitally, staying slim and trim is also one of the most important things you can do for your overall health. Did you know that high blood pressure is twice as common in overweight people? Or that your risk of arthritis increases 9–13 percent for every two pounds of weight you gain, or that gaining as little as eleven to eighteen pounds doubles your chance of developing type 2 diabetes, or that women who gain more than twenty pounds between the age of eighteen and midlife double the risk of developing breast cancer after menopause? It's about far more than looks for vanity's sake; the benefits of staying in shape cover all aspects of a woman's life. You want to enjoy a long and active relationship with your soul mate when you find him—that should be impetus enough!

You might be willing but thinking, Marla, I just don't have the time to exercise, what with my full-time job and the kids and everything else I have to do. Let me tell you, you can't afford *not* to make the time. I work all day at the office, have a husband, a writing career, friends, errands, and so on. Believe me, I understand there don't seem to be enough hours in the day. I slacked off on the workouts for a while and ended up gaining eight pounds. Now I'm back at it, getting up forty-five minutes earlier each morning to take a power walk in the hills, and I've cut out my afternoon snacks and wine in the evening. Otherwise the eight pounds will soon turn into ten, fifteen, and on and on.

Of course you don't want to obsess about your weight, or beat yourself up over extra pounds. I'm sure you all know one of those women who are roughly the size of a twig but still think they're fat. You know, one ones who make everybody miserable with picky ordering at restaurants and refusing to ever eat a real meal. *Puh-leeeze!* Looking and feeling healthy, fit, strong, and sexy is the goal.

Eating healthfully can definitely be a challenge for women on the go, but you can do it! If you stick to Deepak Chopra's advice—"Avoid eating anything with a label on it"—you will be off to an amazing start! Here are some easy, helpful tips you should try if you're not already doing them. These are all things I make a point of doing, and I really feel great!

- Invest in a juicer and make wonderful fresh vegetable and fruit juices right at home.

- Drink plenty of filtered water. Sodas of any kind are terrible for your health and should be cut out of your diet.

- Drink green tea daily. Green tea has powerful antioxidants, catechins that have been shown to fight viruses, slow aging, reduce high blood pressure, lower blood sugar, and help prevent cancer. Green tea also boosts the immune system and helps prevent tooth decay.

• Avoid eating fried foods.

• Incorporate olive oil into your diet.

• If you want to sweeten coffee, cereal, or smoothies, skip the refined sugar and use stevia instead. It can be purchased at any health food store. Stevia, which is a noncaloric herb native to Paraguay that has been used as a sweetener and flavor enhancer for centuries, is sweeter than sugar.

• Cut animal products out of your diet. They are loaded with saturated fats, hormones, and antibiotics. If you don't feel that you can cut them out completely, try to cut down to a couple of times per week. Your body and the animals will thank you.

• Eat goji berries every day. You can buy them at any health-food store. The goji berry is a complete protein loaded with eighteen amino acids including all eight essential amino acids. They contain more than twenty trace minerals and vitamins including iron, zinc, copper, B complex, and vitamins C and E. I used to get a cold every year, especially working in a small office with employees who seemed to get sick all the time, coughing and sneezing. Since I have been eating the goji berries, people can cough near me all they want and I never get sick.

Making healthful and smart changes gradually will get you and keep you on the road to looking and feeling great, which of course will result in attracting a soul mate!

So to answer the original question, "Does he just want an arm piece?" in a way, yes! But that is not all our brothers are looking for in a woman. When interviewing men, there are five other qualities of a perfect partner that continually top the list:

1. *Intelligence.* She doesn't necessarily have to have a college degree, as long as she is bright and can have a stimulating conversation. A woman can be stunning in the looks department, but if she doesn't know who our country's vice president is or where Portugal is located, he won't be inclined to take her to upscale events with his business associates.

2. *Easygoing.* Men love a woman who can go with the flow, someone who is not constantly complaining and pouting. Men want a woman who is open to trying new experiences. If he takes you to an opera or a football game and you can't see straight out of sheer boredom, at least try to pretend you like it, and appreciate his efforts in doing something nice for you.

3. *Has her own interests.* A man likes to know that a woman has things that she is passionate about and involved in other than him. Having your own full and busy day also gives you lots to talk about at the dinner table.

4. *Up on current events.* Men love a woman who knows what is going on in the world. Women in their twenties don't tend to keep up with current events as much as the older gals, but at least find out who the major movers and shakers on the world stage are and have an overview of what's going on.

5. *Good sense of humor.* Being able to laugh and not take yourself too seriously is a critical part of a good relationship.

As you can see, men are generally looking for the whole "package." Good looks and a great body will open the door but only get you so far.

Dating Exercise

Write down five small changes that you can make in your lifestyle that will support a healthier and more interesting you.

1._____

2._____

3._____

4._____

5._____

It's All about the Car!

You can never get enough of what you don't need to make you happy.

—Eric Hoffer

While women bemoan the fact that men only want an arm piece, I feel the need to add a few words about something that all men know most women won't compromise about. I have found that, minor as it may seem, people are extremely fixated, hung up, concerned, obsessed, interested, or downright unreasonable about what kind of car someone drives.

When looking for a life partner, women definitely consider how much money the man makes, his social status, and what types of "goodies" might come with the relationship—including the car! It's the Cinderella dream of finding that Prince to take care of us. Living and working in Los Angeles, I tend to deal with a lot more women looking for a "benefactor," as one of my female clients likes to put it. I am sure that in every city there are many ladies looking for a similar situation. Our society tends to be extremely materialistic. We are constantly bombarded with images in the media of uber-rich celebrities and ads telling us that if we don't drive this car or wear those jeans or carry that handbag, we are not important. Sometimes I wonder whatever happened to loving someone for their amazing character, zest, and enthusiasm for life, or their romantic, trusting heart. Not to mention that being physically attracted to the person is a given! But I don't hear much about all those things—at least not at first. One of the first things many women want to know is, "What does he drive?"

I had lunch with one of my male clients the other day, and we chatted about all sorts of topics as well as dating. I told him that I had just bought a new car. He asked me what kind, and I told him, "It's a Toyota Scion XA in salsa red, and I just love it! It's great on gas, it's small so it's easy to park, and it was a great price."

"Gosh, Marla," he said, "That's a great car for a woman, but can you imagine me as a man in L.A. showing up on a date in a Toyota Scion? The girls wouldn't go for that. I have to have a Mercedes, Porsche, BMW, or something like that."

Sadly, I had to agree, "That is so true. You couldn't get away with it here."

Recently, in Mexico City, I got together with a married woman who told me that she thought my books would do very well in her city, since there are significantly more women than men there, and the dating scene is quite daunting. The women there are also very concerned about what type of car the man drives and what possessions he has, so they often wind up alone rather than "settle." It was an interesting conversation for me, because in Los Angeles we see so many people driving Ferraris, Porsches, Mercedes, even Rolls-Royces and Bentleys, we've become used to it. In Mexico City, due to kidnappings and security risks, people with money need to be low-key and not show off their assets; to do so could be trouble or even fatal. So you don't see flashy cars everywhere like you do in Beverly Hills. Even so, my friend told me, there is a level of acceptable cars a man can drive for a woman to consider going out with him.

In addition to asking about a prospective date's car, I have had many women clients ask me about his income. I do have some ladies who refuse to meet a man who makes less than a million per year, and a few who will only date a man who owns a private jet. Now, keep in mind that these women are not wealthy themselves, nor do they even come from wealthy families. Most are close to broke and struggling, looking for a meal ticket. They have seen celebrities jetting off to exotic destinations, eating at the best restaurants, and shopping at the designer stores. They figure that since they are attractive, they want the same lifestyle and will settle for nothing less. They go and get the fake breasts, the fake hair color, the Botox, the liposuction, fake nails, and a fake personality. Then they build a fake profile, which includes lying about their job, as well as their age and weight.

I tell women that if they want to date a multimillionaire or billionaire, go for it. But they must realize that this rare species usually dates only the most gorgeous and in-demand women. These men have big money to offer, and the women have world-class looks to offer in return.

I completely understand a woman not wanting to get into a situation where she would be supporting a man while he's trying to become a rock star or deciding what to do with his life, but the men who join the service I work for all are well established in their careers and looking to complete the package with someone special with whom to spend the rest of their lives. Ladies, take my word for it, the make and model of a car will not guarantee a great relationship, or even that the guy has a lot of money! More people are in debt trying to look the part by buying or leasing a fancy car!

Thank goodness my friend Renee was not in that mindset when she met her husband. When he arrived at her apartment to pick her up for their first date, he was driving an unfortunate red broken-down 1993 Daihatsu that he called "the Predator." Had Renee been a snob, she wouldn't have seen him again, but he was so charming, caring, fun, and sexy that he could have picked her up in a rickshaw, she later told me. On the other hand, I recently interviewed a twenty-seven-year-old struggling model/actress who told me she only flies private. The last man she dated had a private jet and now she is spoiled. "I just can't go back to flying commercial!" In the meantime, she is missing out on meeting some wonderful, quality, successful, commitment-minded men just because she is now a spoiled brat.

I took a phone call a few weeks ago from a former male client with whom I still keep in touch. When I picked up the phone, he said he needed my advice. He told me that about a month earlier, he had had a second date with a woman that seemed to go pretty well. They just had a nice dinner, nothing special, and he hadn't spoken to her since. Then she called him out of the blue and told him that she needed four thousand dollars to pay some bills. He was in complete shock and didn't know what to say to her. He was out of town at a conference when she phoned, so he just said, "Well, I am out of town and can't really talk now." She then asked him to go to Western Union and wire her the money!

He managed to get her off the phone with some excuse and then called me in a panic, wondering what to do. He told me that he had never had such a request from a woman before, and did not feel comfortable giving her the money, but he didn't want to be rude either. Well, can you guess my advice? I told him not to return her call and not to accept any of her future calls. I felt so embarrassed that I was the one who originally introduced him to this woman.

It's All about the Lips

*Do you love me because I am beautiful or am I beautiful
because you love me?*

—Oscar Hammerstein II

What is going on these days with the big inflated lips?
I might be seeing more than the norm because I live in Los
Angeles, but I have heard that this look is cropping up
nationwide. Whom are the ladies doing this for? If they
think men like it, I want every woman reading this to know
that men *don't* like those big fake duck lips! And if they are
doing it for other women, they also think it looks ridiculous. Those lips will not make you look younger, they will
only make you look like a woman with big lips. Angelina
Jolie won the genetic lottery. She is gorgeous in every way
and she has natural, full, kissable lips. If you weren't born
with them, deal with the lips the good Lord gave you. Please.

Recently, I was sitting at the piano bar at a local restaurant in Beverly Hills with a single male friend of mine. He
was pointing out women that he found attractive, hoping
maybe I would be able to fix him up. Every time a woman
walked in with the big lips, huge implants, and collagen-
injected face that looked like it was about to explode, he
would look at me and roll his eyes. "Not in a million years
would I be interested in that."

Everyone wants to look good and feel attractive, but
the fact of life is that we are going to age. We are supposed

to, that is what nature intended. By all means stay in shape, dress sharp, and get the latest hairstyle, but the plastic surgery look is just that, a "look," which at first glance tells people that you are old but don't want to be, so you messed up your face to try to look younger. In fact, the procedures actually did the opposite and attracted attention to the fact that you are insecure with yourself and trying to pretend to be something you are not.

I realize that there is a lot of pressure on women to look hot and youthful since the media is constantly bombarding us with unrealistic images of beauty, but keep in mind that is all about selling products and making money for cosmetic and clothing companies. Our true selves are inside, encased in the flesh. Develop your intellect, personality, and your spiritual side. Become so darn fascinating that you radiate beauty and light from the inside out instead of trying to rearrange everything on the outside! In an interview with Oprah, Eckhart Tolle talked about the ego and how difficult it is for extremely good-looking people to age, because they have had so much attention for so long that they cannot handle losing it. It was quite humorous when he mentioned that luckily he had personally never had that problem.

Certainly, aging is a humbling process. I used to wonder how I would feel when I was older and not getting the kind of attention that I attracted when I was younger. I did have one wake-up call about four years ago when I was on a business trip in Scottsdale with another matchmaker I worked with named Lindsay. She was twenty-four and could have passed for eighteen. The two of us were at a

Mexican restaurant sitting at the bar having margaritas. I was dressed real cute in a sexy sundress. Then one of the busboys asked me in Spanish if Lindsay was my daughter!

I don't have any kids and that was the first time that anyone had ever asked me if I was someone's mother! I was shocked and hurt. I didn't think I looked old enough to have a grown daughter. I rationalized it by telling myself that in Mexico people often have kids quite young, so he probably thought that I had had her when I was a teenager (yeah, right). I guess that I could have freaked out and run to the plastic surgeon, but would it really change anything? I decided to embrace my changing face and body and appreciate all that it has done for me in the past, while really concentrating on my other qualities such as my intellect and creativity. It is a very rich and satisfying way to feel and live. I have also noticed that since I have increasingly concentrated on the inner in the past few years, I no longer need reassurance from strangers that I'm good enough, because I look and feel exceptional. I know that I am exceptional just for being me!

Dating Exercise

List three exceptional traits you have besides your looks.

1._____

2. _____

3. _____

It's All about the Hair!

I want to let you in on a little secret. Maybe you have heard that men just *love* long hair on women. It's true, they do! They feel that it looks more feminine. For most of my thirties while living in Chicago, I had short hair in every different style. I did the sleek Victoria Beckham bob, the choppy Meg Ryan in *French Kiss* look, and even the Sharon Stone *Muse* look, and I never lacked for dates. Not one man told me that they did not like my hair. I even received many compliments, telling me how sexy I was.

Needless to say, I was shocked when I moved to L.A., married a Latin man, and learned that short hair was not going to fly. I have very thin, dry hair, and if it grows past the middle of my neck, it is actually see-through because it is so thin! Naturally, I prefer to wear it short. But it doesn't matter how scraggly and ridiculous it looks, as long as it is not short, my husband is in heaven. I did grow it all the way down my back for him once, but I wound up putting my hair in a ponytail all the time because it was so raggedy. Of course, he thought it looked amazing! (Fortunately, my husband also loves me with no makeup. I'm actually very lucky that I can look like what I consider to be a wreck, but he still thinks I look like a goddess.) The most puzzling thing to me is that my husband loves it when I wear my hair up in a French twist or ponytail. I don't see the difference in those styles compared to short hair. Eventually, I couldn't take it anymore! Now, I manage to keep my hair just at the middle of my neck, and he seems okay with its length—after much discussion.

I once had a boss who required that all women in the office wear their hair down. We were not allowed to wear a sophisticated French twist or ponytail, as our boss believed it would make a difference to the potential male clients. It used to really burn us ladies up! How dare a man tell us how to wear our hair! Still, when interviewing men, I must admit that 90 percent tell me that they prefer longer hair on a woman. I have asked many men exactly why they prefer this, and they all tell me the same things: "Long hair is more feminine." "If the woman has short hair, I feel like I'm with a guy." "Long hair is a turn-on."

Personally, I don't get it, I mean if the woman is in shape, stylish, and has a great cut, what is the difference? But it does make a big difference to the men and it's a small enough adjustment to make, so you might want to keep this in mind on your next trip to the hairdresser.

FIVE

Seek Abundance, Not Money

Even if the five billion human beings that inhabit the earth become millionaires, without inner development there cannot be peace or lasting happiness. Some people may be very rich, but we often find that they are not happy at all. Affection, love, and compassion are some of the most important elements in our life.

—The Dalai Lama

Sometimes I get a little tough with my clients and push them to examine what they truly want out of a relationship in their lives and what motives lie behind their desires. Even after all of these years in the business, I still find myself bewildered when I meet a gal who is young, beautiful, educated, intelligent, creative, with a wonderful personality, but doesn't want to work. Her sole purpose in life is to find someone to "help her out financially." I see these wonderful women dating "professionally" and going from "relationship" to "relationship" for years, looking to land the big fish.

In the meantime, they are not building a future for themselves. They are not getting valuable work experience or building any funds for retirement. The scary part about this plan is if they have not landed the big catch by a certain age, it's too late. When she's in her forties, most of the wealthy guys will be looking for younger women. Besides having no partner, she will be stuck with nothing and no skills to get into a good career. She may also have missed out on having children and be frantically seeking a partner, hoping it's not too late to get pregnant.

Almost all of the men I interview tell me that they are looking for a woman who has something going on in her life, something that she is passionate about. She doesn't need to have a PhD or own her own business, but they want to know that she is not just looking for a meal ticket or waiting for him to get home from work because she has nothing to do.

The days when women were raised to aspire only to finding a husband, having children, and tending to the house are long gone. And why would we want to go back to that era anyway? Today a woman has so much more control over her own life and destiny; she is not at the mercy of a man for her very survival.

Think about how blessed and lucky you are just to have the money to buy this book! Most of the people on this planet live in poverty. When you go out to a lovely dinner with a date, you might think, "This guy is a bore, and he picked *this* restaurant? What bad taste." Meanwhile, how many millions of women would be deeply grateful for a hot meal out in a restaurant? You are so blessed to have food, shelter, loved ones, some money in your pocket, a car to get around in. Feel grateful for the little things in life, because the "little" things in *your* life are enormous riches to the vast majority of humans on Earth!

I am not suggesting that you settle for less or not have the level of lifestyle you dream of. I am encouraging and inviting you to realize the intelligence, wisdom, creativity, and strength within you and from that point of power vibrationally invite a true partner into your life. Seek a true love based on caring, respect, and teamwork. Don't ever count on someone else to come and rescue you. How exciting and fulfilling it is to know that you can take care of yourself, to know that you can buy yourself a car or take yourself on a trip! Step up to the plate and live your life to the fullest, constantly learning and experiencing new things and at the same time emotionally vibrating at such a high frequency that you will attract your soul mate into your life. If you do this, I guarantee that you can't go wrong!

The most important thing for a woman to do is to look out for herself. Have enough concern, respect, and love for yourself to make sure that you will be okay with or without a man. I remember chatting years ago in Chicago with a girlfriend of mine who was engaged to be married. The relationship was volatile and she clearly chose this man because he came from a wealthy family. He was expected to inherit a large amount of money when his grandmother died.

I asked her one day if she had a retirement account. She looked at me like I was crazy and said, "Oh, no, Garrett is going to take care of all that. I don't need one of my own." Well, Garrett broke off the engagement the next year. My friend never did open a retirement account, and she still isn't married. Except now she's in her forties.

Ladies, if you do not have a retirement plan at your work, whatever your age, please march yourself down to your bank, or call a financial consultant and open up an IRA, an individual retirement account. Contribute to it every month. You will thank me later. It is so easy to let the years go by without saving anything. Do you really want to be working like a dog into your seventies and eighties? That is what you will be doing unless you take action now.

I love Suze Orman's book *Women & Money: Owning the Power to Control Your Destiny*. Another fabulous one is *Smart Women Finish Rich*, by David Bach. Please get one or both and read them! Don't count on a man. Even if you do marry a rich one, he could cheat on you, leave you, die, become disabled, lose all of his money, or treat you so badly that you want to leave. Always have your own projects going and your own money. You will feel secure, powerful, and in control.

I recently heard some news about an acquaintance of mine, a man in his mid-forties—handsome, brilliant, and wealthy. He was a finance guy and a pillar in his community. A huge number of people in the community invested their savings in his company. Something went wrong and he lost everyone's money, including his own. He was so ashamed that he felt he could not face the people whose money he'd lost. He committed suicide, leaving behind devastated family and friends. I mention this to emphasize that while money is important, it can also be a heavy burden.

What Really Matters

To me, no amount of money compares to the value of happiness and peace of mind.

I am writing this chapter now from Mexico City. My mother-in-law passed away this morning. Her body was brought to the house a couple of hours ago, and we are waiting for the family to arrive this evening when we will gather around the coffin with seven nuns reciting prayers and singing. It is early June, and the weather is beautiful. I am sitting on the patio among the trees and can hear the birds singing.

When my husband and I found out that his mother had had a stroke, we got on the plane from L.A. the next morning. My husband has four siblings, and they have children. There are also many cousins and aunts and uncles around us. The circumstances are very sad and painful, but what we found out is that our family is united, strong, and supportive. Over the several days and nights we all spent together waiting at the hospital, taking all of our meals together and sitting at the house, we all expressed our love and appreciation for one another. I will be going back to my life in Hollywood a bit more humble, caring, and sensitive, with a renewed sense of what is truly important in life.

Get clear on what really matters to you. Your life is meant to be enjoyed, treasured, and experienced to the fullest. It is our relationships with each other and the love we give and receive that is of any value—not the brand of a handbag, model of a car, or size of a house. Money has an important place and can make life more comfortable, but it is not the answer to everything. Look toward what you can give, whom you can love, and what you can share, and you will be richer than you ever imagined!

Dating Exercise

Write down three steps that you can take now to feel more secure and to rely on yourself.

1._____

2._____

3._____

Communication Is the Key

Any man who does not know the power of the word is
behind the times.

—Florence Scovel Shinn,
The Game of Life and How to Play It

You'd Think We'd Have It Figured Out by Now!

Lance and Misty have been dating exclusively for two years. For the past year or so, they've talked about marriage in vague terms such as, "Wouldn't you just love to have a house in the country?" or "I've always wanted a big family and a dog and a cat," but no firm details have been set. Misty knows in her heart that she and Lance are meant to be together, but she wants Lance to make the first move, so she hints around about being engaged. For instance, when they are walking by a jewelry store, she stops at the window display and says to Lance, "Aren't those rings beautiful?" When they discuss their friends Alex and Cindy, Misty says, "They're so lucky to be getting married this summer. Don't you think the beach is a beautiful place to get married?"

Valentine's Day is coming up in a few weeks, and Misty is convinced that Lance is going to show up with a ring. Although Lance is not opposed to marriage, and figures he and Misty will "tie the knot" at some point, the thought hasn't even occurred to him to get Misty a ring for Valentine's Day. Instead, he plans to surprise her by taking her to that trendy new Italian restaurant that just opened downtown. She's wanted to try it, and they can share a nice bottle of wine.

Valentine's Day arrives, and Lance and Misty arrive at the restaurant. Misty is thrilled because she is convinced that her ring is going to show up in her wine glass or napkin. Of course, no ring shows up. Misty starts getting tense. "Maybe," she tells herself, "he just doesn't want to make a scene in public. He'll probably want to take a little walk afterward and pop the question then."

After dinner Lance announces, "Let's get back. There's a great movie on tonight I've been wanting to see."

Misty's mood darkens further. "Maybe the ring will be in the popcorn bowl," she tells herself desperately. No ring shows up. Misty is furious. Her mood soon becomes apparent to Lance.

"What's the matter?" Lance asks, but Misty is too angry by now to tell him. "Well, if everything's okay then," he says, "I guess I'll get going now." He awkwardly pecks her on the cheek and leaves.

Misty is in tears. "He should know what I want!" she fumes to herself. "Obviously, he's never going to pop the question. Tomorrow I'm going to send him a 'Dear John' letter and move on! I'm just wasting my life with a man who is never going to marry me!"

Mind Reading Is Not a Communication Skill!

Communication is the way we convey our hopes, expectations, feelings, dreams, and fears. They are expressed through our words, our facial expressions, our body language, our tone of voice, and our mannerisms. Successful dating relies heavily on good communication skills. Communicating effectively during the dating process will help lead you to your goal of having a successful relationship. When you practice your communication skills while dating, you'll have a better chance of maintaining your relationship once you find your soul mate. A wise person once said, "To love a person is to learn the song that is in their heart and to sing it to them when they have forgotten."

If you find that your dates and relationships are often failing because your expectations are not being met, it's time to ask yourself how well you've been doing at conveying your expectations. If you are not up-front about what you want from the relationship, you only set yourself up for disappointment when your partner fails to provide it. It doesn't mean that your partner doesn't want to meet your expectations; it just means that he might not have been aware of them in the first place. By learning how to communicate effectively, you'll have a much better chance of "hooking" and keeping the person who is right for you.

Lance and Misty are a perfect example of a couple that belongs together but is about to throw away a good relationship due to poor communication. Both of them want marriage as a long-term goal, but they failed to discuss it openly. Misty threw around vague hints and expected Lance to read her thoughts, while Lance just tabled the discussion and figured the issue would resolve itself somehow in the future. Lance and Misty had an otherwise good relationship and plenty in common, but their lack of communication on this important issue caused a rift between them.

Unfortunately, people can rarely read each other's minds. Yet how often do we expect our partner to do just that? Yes, your partner should be familiar with your likes and dislikes after you have dated for a few years, but that doesn't make him a mind reader. You still need to express your needs clearly and often. Poor communication is often characterized by the use of threats, the "silent treatment," yelling, and recriminations. If you and your partner find yourselves using these techniques a lot, it's the first sign that your communication skills have broken down (or were never present in the first place!). Communication is crucial at all stages of a relationship, whether you are going on a first date or have been together for many years. Anytime communications break down, the relationship is in danger of failing.

Dating Exercise

List five ways that you can communicate more clearly when in a relationship or on a date.

1._____

2._____

3._____

4._____

5._____

Mixed Messages, Jumping to Conclusions, and General Chaos!

The human mind (ego) can play some pretty nasty tricks on us at times. Often I will give to a gentleman info on a new match with her phone number and he will call her, excited to meet a new lady and hoping that she will finally be "the one." A day or two or three will pass, and I get a phone call from him notifying me that his match has not returned his phone call. He will go on and on with possible scenarios as to why she did not return his call. "Maybe she got back with her ex, or she is not serious about find-ing a relationship, or she probably did not like my voice on the phone or my description." I sit there patiently listen-ing, then give my usual response, "The fact is, you don't have any idea why she hasn't returned your call, so why make up these elaborate reasons and stress yourself out? Let me call her and find out, and I will let you know."

When I call or e-mail the woman and ask what is going on, it usually turns out that she was just swamped with work, had family in from out of town, or was out of town and was planning to call him as soon as she had a free moment to relax and talk to him. She did not go back to her ex, dislike his voice, or any of the hundred reasons he came up with.

It is very important to get out of our own way and not to listen to the ego—the voice in the head that is constantly creating drama and scenarios that may or may not be true but for sure will drive you crazy. A story comes to mind about one of my husband's best friends since childhood, Alex. When my husband and I got married in Mexico City, invita-tions went out to all of his friends there. Alex received his, but didn't even open it because he figured that the wedding was going to take place in Los Angeles where we lived, and he didn't have the time or money to make that trip. My hus-band was hurt that Alex did not contact him or show up at the wedding since he only lived a few miles from the church.

My husband didn't speak to him for about five years over this incident. It was only recently that we learned what had happened (Alex jumping to the conclusion that the wedding was in L.A.) on our recent trip to Mexico for my mother-in-law's funeral. Alex reached out when he heard the sad news, and we met his wife and him for breakfast, over which we finally heard the whole story. I remembered my father telling me as a child, "Never assume." How right he was.

Below are some examples of situations with my clients that illustrate how people often jump to conclusions. Doing so only perpetuates the frustration and negativity around dating in general, the very last thing you need!

This feedback was written after the couple had gone out on two dates:

Hi Marla,

Update on Marissa. Believe it or not, I never saw her again. We had a fantastic first date. I mean it really clicked. I tried to play it cool, but she grabbed my hand to hold it while walking to her car. She told me to kiss her. We then made plans for our next date. Over the next two weeks, things came up with her, for example, at work, with family, and then sickness. But she kept insisting how much she wanted to see me again. We were all set to see each other last Sunday, but then she called and told me she had the chicken pox. I said something like, "I'm sorry you are sick, let's try to do something when you are feeling better." Midweek I phoned. She never returned my call. I have not talked to her since. I don't get it? I feel like I got teased. I am asking you to contact her and get feedback for me.

Thank you.

Nathan

I did get feedback from Marissa. She told me that she really likes Nathan but she has been very sick and planned to call him as soon as she was feeling better. So Nathan jumped to his own conclusions and felt teased and frustrated when, in fact, there was nothing wrong, Marissa was just ill. If someone does not get back to you right away, keep yourself busy with other things. Don't jump to conclusions, because you really have no idea what the other person is thinking.

Was this next couple even in the same text message conversation or on the same date?

Hi Marla,

I finally was able to go out with Andy last night. His age was great, he was really nice and fun, but he was not my type physically at all . . . his looks and slicked-back hair. I go more for a rugged or pretty boy. He was nice at dinner . . . but a little self-absorbed with his talk on music and the band, but really a gentleman. The only issue I had is that he texted me this evening and told me he had a great time and I let him know that I did too but would like to be friends and he was quite rude in his response . . . kind of put me down . . . not a graceful loser so to speak. I am just telling you this in case you give the guys guidance about how to date because that is definitely a put-off and I wouldn't even be friends with him at this point. You are very close . . . just someone a little more with a sensitive spot perhaps? I am interested in meeting the right guy. Thanks sweetie and take care,

Judy

I e-mailed Andy and gave him her feedback. He was totally confused and sent me this e-mail:

> Wasn't rude, just honest. Here is the exact texting:
> Me: Nice meeting you last night!
> Her: Thx. U2! Would love to be friends.
> Me: Thanks anyway, didn't really feel a connection either. Good luck 2 you though . . .
> Her: Glad we're on the same page. Take care!
> Don't think that was rude, right? Again, she was just so into herself, talked about herself and her business the entire time, not really asking me any questions or even caring. Anyway, just wanted you to know how the text went so you can judge for yourself.
> Thanks,
> Andy

So while Judy felt that Andy talked too much about his music and the band, Andy felt that Judy was self-absorbed, talking the whole time about herself. Judy interpreted Andy's good luck text as being a sore loser. With this couple, the chemistry was clearly lacking, but I do find it very interesting that they both felt that the other spoke mostly about her/himself.

This next couple went out together twice. For the second date, they went to the mall. Nicki said that Arnold offered to take her shopping, which she interpreted as "He's paying." She came into my office all upset that she ended up buying a $300 coat and a $150 dress that she could not afford, and was going to have to return the clothes.

This is his take on it:

Marla,

I did not offer to take her shopping. I asked her what she was doing on Sunday and she said that she was going to the Grove to buy gifts, so I told her maybe we should meet up there and hang out. I never offered to buy her anything, but I did buy her a $260 pair of jeans, which she did not even thank me for! She was not at all interested in me. She did not even ask one question about me. On Friday night she made up an excuse and left me at 10:45 p.m.

Since Sunday she has been calling me ten times and demanding that I go buy her the stuff she has on hold!! When she was trying on the clothes and asking my opinion, I kept telling her to buy it only if she could afford it! She only wanted me to buy her the clothes and did not have any interest in being with me. I would have rather spent time cleaning my house. What did she think I am—her father or her sugar daddy? Even after I got home I decided to go ahead and buy the clothes for her. I texted her to tell her that, but she didn't even have the decency to text me back that night and say thank-you, she texted me yesterday only to ask me what happened!!!

I talked to Arnold and told him his big mistake was to agree to go shopping with a girl on a second date. Shopping trips are for after you have been dating a while or are in a relationship. I have seen too many shopping dates go bad.

This feedback from Gina is interesting. She went out with Paul a few days before Valentine's Day.

Marla,

He was nice, but talked mostly about himself. Asked for a Valentine's date twenty minutes after I met him. Tried to hold my hand under the table. It was really uncomfortable. And he tried to kiss me on the mouth after dinner. He's nice, but for me that is a bit too much. If he had been more interested in me and less touchy-feely, I would have felt more comfortable. He seems a little in a rush to hop into a new relationship. I hope this feedback helps.

Tammy

When I gave Paul this feedback, he was surprised and said that Tammy was the one who grabbed his hand from across the table. He did ask her if she had plans for that Thursday; it just so happened that it was Valentine's Day. And as far as trying to kiss her on the lips, he said that she kissed him on the cheek while waiting for the valet to bring the car. I hear this type of feedback quite often—the woman feels that the man was too touchy-feely, and the man says that she initiated it. Men can often interpret a touch on the arm, revealing clothing, or sitting very close as an invitation for more intimate contact. Set your boundaries from the beginning if you are not sure about chemistry by being sweet and friendly but keeping an appropriate distance and your hands to yourself.

Do you notice a common thread that runs through so

much of the feedback from both the men and the women? He/she talked mostly about him/herself. They didn't seem interested in me. I hear this so often—especially when alcohol is involved. That's when people tend to really spill their guts about their past, flaws, doubts, and fears and take over the conversation. But vino aside, a seeming lack of interest is one of the most common complaints I hear. Everyone wants to feel important, interesting, captivating, attractive, and noticed. Listening and really showing an interest in the person who is sitting across from you is crucial. Even if you know that you have no romantic chemistry and do not plan to see this person again, why not go ahead and practice your listening skills? You just might learn something as well!

Hi Marla,

After several nice phone calls, chatting on instant messenger, text messages etc. over the past couple of weeks, I finally had dinner with Alexis last night in Beverly Hills. I was really excited to meet her since we had nice conversations beforehand and she seemed charming and down-to-earth. Maybe I am totally off, but I felt like she was not interested and was bored throughout the dinner. She looked down at her food most of the time and did not make much eye contact, did not smile that much, did not ask me anything about myself. The conversation felt forced as I was asking her all of the questions. She also took two hours to eat her entrée, king crab. It was weird because I really wanted there to be a connection. Maybe I am reading too much into a first date, so any feedback that you receive will be much appreciated. Anyway, thank-you for the introduction as she seems like a very nice person, but there did not seem to be chemistry or a connection.

Brendon

I e-mailed Alexis this feedback (condensed), and this was her take on the date:

"I liked him. The only time I didn't look at him was when I was trying to get the meat out of my Dungeness crab. I did ask him questions, such as where his family lives, how many siblings he has, how far is his work from where he lives, etc. But if I go out with him again I'm just going to be me, not change myself to his liking and start staring at him all night and feel the need to lead the conversation."

This is a clear case of miscommunication. They both liked each other, but Alexis was acting a bit coy, and Brendon wanted some signals that she was interested.

I matched Emily with a guy named Brad. I had told her that Brad was extremely cultured, well traveled, and intelligent and that he was looking for a cultured, intelligent lady as well. He called her to touch base and to ask her out on a date for Friday night. He asked Emily what part of town she lived in. Then he suggested that they go to eat at a place in West Hollywood called Barney's Beanery, which is a super-casual place with pool tables and a huge beer list. Emily was appalled. She suggested a couple of other places, and he told her that he would pick her up and decide from there.

When Friday night arrived, he took her to an upscale trendy Mexican restaurant. Emily's feedback to me was that she couldn't believe that a guy would even suggest taking her to a dive. I said that the Mexican place was fabulous and actually one of my favorite restaurants in town. She said that wasn't good enough for her. She said that she expects to be taken to a five-star restaurant on a first date. She also mentioned that she did not like his shoes. She was disgusted and said that he was low-class and she would never see him again.

When I told Brad that Emily didn't care for his restaurant suggestions, he laughed and said that he often does that on the first phone conversation. He will tell the lady that he likes Barney's Beanery, or sometimes he'll mix it up and say that he wants to take her to Pink's (a hot dog stand) or Carney's (a hamburger joint on Sunset located in an old train car) just to gauge her reaction and to see if she is easygoing and has a sense of humor. He had no intention of actually taking her there.

I knew for a fact that Brad was a gentleman, because I had feedback from another lady about where he had taken her and how he had gone out of his way to bring her dark chocolates and her favorite flower. I told Emily that Brad was joking and that I knew he was upscale, but she was firm on her impression and said that if a man doesn't take her to the best places from the get-go, she will not see him again. I told her straight out that she was too high maintenance and unreasonable. She said, "I know, that's why I am single. But I won't change my mind!"

There was clearly some miscommunication here. That, combined with Brad's wicked sense of humor and Emily's uptight attitude, spoiled what could possibly have been a great evening.

SEVEN

The Nitty-Gritty

If you want a committed man, look in a mental hospital.

—Mae West

How Do You See Men?

It's easy to fall into the trap of becoming frustrated, bitter, or negative and start using language about men that will keep you locked in a vicious cycle. How many times have we women said or heard other women say, "Men are jerks," "Men are pigs," or "I'm so sick of men!" Ladies, I want to invite you to change your language about our brothers. They are just as confused about things as we are. If you wouldn't want something said about you, don't say it about them. Changing your language and thoughts about men to the positive will change your experience and outlook. Remember, what you expect to get out of dating is pretty much what you *will* get.

Here are five positive affirmations that you can start with to begin changing how you see men:

1. The men that I meet are considerate, kind, and caring.

2. The men that I meet are fun, intelligent, and interesting.

3. The men that I meet are commitment-minded and have high integrity.

4. I appreciate my brothers and wish them nothing but the best.

5. I am blessed to have good experiences with men.

Dating Exercise

Create your own affirmations.

1. _____

2. _____

3. _____

Where the Boys Are

Given all the millions of people and possibilities in the world, where does one go to find a soul mate? How about the supermarket? Lurking in the frozen food section? Fondling the fruits? Standing in the checkout line? Your soul mate could be in the most unlikely, everyday place!

Believe me, I know it's not easy to approach a stranger. When I was single and had moved back to Los Angeles from Chicago, I realized that this was a much different, more difficult environment in which to meet people. In Los Angeles, people spend much of their time in their cars; very few people are walking down the street. I saw cute guys all the time, driving or jogging by, but there was no way to meet them. The online thing wasn't for me. I was sure there must be a better way than chasing after cars or joggers.

In *Excuse Me, Your Soul Mate Is Waiting,* I talk about how looking may be the equivalent of losing. Though women should not be desperate and constantly out looking for the right one, at the same time Prince Charming is not going to come knocking on your door either. It's essential that you get out and put yourself in a position to meet members of the opposite sex.

Here are fifteen ideas and places to get you in front of the eligible men you are hoping to get to know a bit better!

1. Got a dog? Try the dog park; there is no better way to bond than over discussions about pedigree or training tips.

2. Start drinking coffee. Have you ever noticed the cuties hanging out at your local Starbucks or Coffee Bean with their laptops or just relaxing with a cup of java?

3. The gym. Are you sick of me telling you to get those hot cross buns firmed up? Need some more motivation? Scope out the available physically fit men spending their evenings pumping iron.

4. Friends. Have a powwow with your closest amigas and put out the word that you are looking for "the one." They can fix you up and act as your "agent" in the game of love. Or throw one of those fun parties where everyone brings an ex that they would like to recycle!

5. Men love cars. Where to meet all kinds of men who love cars? Car shows, NASCAR races, the Indy 500—you get the idea.

6. Are you a wine connoisseur? Many men now are really into wine and have wonderful wine cellars to fill. Join a wine tasting club or class. Flirt and mingle over a marvelous merlot.

7. Are you a bookworm? Meet like-minded men at your local bookstore. Peruse the travel section, and you just might be planning your next trip with a new man over a cappuccino at the bookstore café.

8. Volunteer. This is an often overlooked way to meet a great guy with a big heart. Maybe you love animals or support fundraising for a hospice or are passionate about saving the whales. Every charity has opportunities to get involved, and they are a great way for single people to meet. It is also a more comfortable way to get to know someone since conversation is natural and most likely necessary.

9. The Apple Store. My husband's favorite destination is the Apple Store. He is a committed Mac guy, as he calls himself, and loves to check out all of the latest features and computers. On all of my trips there with him, I notice the abundance of the male species.

10. Home Depot. If you like a manly man, check out the hardware stores to meet handy men.

11. Have a high IQ? Join MENSA and hook up with a brainiac at one of their events or parties in your area.

12. Whole Foods. I have never seen more good-looking people in one supermarket than at Whole Foods. I even ran into that dreamboat Leonardo DiCaprio at the West Hollywood location.

13. Film festivals. Every major city has one, or even better, go to Sundance or Cannes and mingle with the creative types or producers.

14. Learn to play pool. There's nothing sexier to a guy than a woman in a tight pair of jeans leaning over and announcing "Eight ball in the side pocket!"

15. Are you a ham? Karaoke bars are still quite popular and a lot of fun.

Are You a Drama Queen?

Just the idea of dating can bring up thoughts and feelings of drama. I was a gigantic drama queen in my twenties and, sadly, well into my thirties as well. I used to thrive on the excitement of it all. It made life so interesting, wondering whether the guy I went out with or met one night would call, whether we would end up in a relationship. I would get so hyped up on the whole thing that there were times when I was attracted to someone new, that I would lose ten pounds in a week! I know, that part doesn't sound so bad, does it? I couldn't sleep, eat, or think of anything else. It was exciting at the time, but now I just think of that kind of drama as exhausting! I did start tapering off around the age of thirty-eight. Hey, a little late, I know, but at least I am drama-free now.

Working as a matchmaker, I get to hear all of the feedback and do plenty of counseling as well, and I hear a lot of drama going on. I recently matched a new female client, Shelly, with a guy named Ron. Unfortunately, she had some scheduling problems and had to push the date back a couple of hours. He said fine, and came to her house to pick her up at the appointed time but could not get through the security gate. He called her, but she didn't answer, so he turned around and went home. She finally texted him to say that she was home but did not hear his call. He texted her back something nasty, which led to exchanges that went back and forth for a couple of days. Shelly called me and said that she had never had a worse experience and was fuming and stressed out about it.

What needless drama! The whole thing was a misunderstanding and should have been nipped in the bud with an apology. After getting a nasty text from Ron, Shelly should have ignored it and let me know immediately. But she perpetuated the drama by responding, then getting angry and frustrated when there was no need to. It was really not a big deal, but she made it out to be, therefore being a drama queen.

Drama queens are nothing new, but there are some drama kings out there as well. I know a guy named Tad who continuously puts himself in drama-filled relationships. He has been seeing a woman named Cindy on and off for the past two years. She has all sorts of problems, including drug and alcohol abuse, but something about Cindy keeps Tad coming back for more, over and over again. Tad recently met a lovely woman named Samantha who is warm, charming, and intelligent, and has her act together. Samantha adores Tad, but he isn't sure if he will stay with her because of the lingering attraction for Cindy.

Dating should be fun and interesting. It's a great way to meet new people, expand your social circle, and make contacts. Dating should not be full of stress and drama, dragging out unpleasant situations or worrying yourself to death. If you can take the drama out of dating, you will have a lot more fun and certainly up your chances of getting into a great relationship.

Dating Exercise

What can you do to live with less drama? List three things to help free you of dating drama.

1._____

2._____

3._____

Date Like a Guy

There are some areas in dating and in life where women can sure benefit by taking a lesson from men. John

Gray says men are from Mars and women are from Venus, and I happen to agree. So let's take a look at what we can learn from our Martian brothers, shall we?

Men are not drama queens—at least, straight men aren't. They keep their dramas and dating disasters to themselves. They want to be brave and show no weakness. Women often remark about their partners, "It's like pulling teeth to get him to talk about his problems." By nature, men are controlled, competitive, and defensive. They hide their emotions to stay in control. From the time they are little boys, men are taught to "act like a man" or told that "men don't cry." Women tend to love to rehash every aspect of their lives, especially their relationships, so much so that many even write books and blogs about their experiences!

If a man has a problem, he will withdraw and take care of business. Women tend to spill their guts to a man on a first or second date and tell them everything from their financial woes to their physical ailments. Women are hardwired to talk and "get out" our feelings, which might be one of the reasons why we live longer. We don't hold things in. But we can learn to tone this tendency down. If you really need to express yourself, you can write in a journal or talk to a therapist, spiritual counselor, or girlfriend. In her book *Enchanted Love*, Marianne Williamson writes, "There's nothing more powerful than a woman who knows how to contain her power and not let it leak, standing firmly within it in mystery and silence. A woman who talks too much sheds her allure."

Men aren't ready to take care of all of your problems,

clean your house, run your errands, and rub your feet after the first date. Men generally take care of themselves first. For a man, listening to a woman's problems is a lot of work, because he feels like he has no choice but to solve all them. Women are naturally nurturing and caregivers. It is a wonderful quality to be caring and loving, but don't be afraid to be a bit selfish, take care of yourself first, and let the man fend for himself.

A woman often believes that the more she does for a man, the more he will appreciate her and want to be with her. Not so. He will probably be grateful to you, but he won't respect you. And he will start expecting you to take care of all the details all of the time. When in early stages of dating, never do for a man what he can do for himself or hire someone to do. You are not a maid, caterer, errand runner, or Laundromat. You have a life and a career to tend to as well. Of course, it is great to reciprocate if he is taking you out a lot, be a classy person like you would with a girlfriend, but there is no need to act like his mommy and jump in and take care of everything.

Men usually don't go exclusive with a woman after one date. They want to keep their options open and see what else is out there. I am always a bit surprised when a female client calls me up and says, "Marla, don't match me up anymore, I just met someone and we really hit it off, he's everything that I'm looking for, thanks." Or even worse, when I match a woman with one of my male clients and after the first date, she doesn't want to meet anyone else, but I know for a fact that he is still dating to see with whom he feels the most chemistry. I tell these ladies to date like a man and keep their options open. If it doesn't work out with this guy who is everything you are looking for, you will still be out there meeting people and have a few irons in the fire. You won't feel as hurt or disappointed if he moves on when you have other options.

Men don't talk about their relationships or where things are going. They are more into action, not words. I personally don't believe in love at first sight; however, I do believe in lust at first sight. Just see how things go, let him prove himself to you, make sure he has the qualities you are looking for in another person. And if you have to ask where the relationship is going, well, it's goin' nowhere.

I hear women all the time refer to their boyfriend or talk about how they are in a relationship with a guy, and they just met him three weeks ago! Until you have been dating exclusively for at least a few months, you are not in a relationship. You are dating the guy. I remember talking to one of my girlfriends once about the guy she was dating and she said testily, "We're not dating, we're *together.*" Oh, *excuse me,* I thought. They weren't married, living together, or engaged, so I would call that dating.

Men don't overanalyze things, including their dates. Women try to figure out what the guy meant when he said this or that, or what it meant that he called at a certain time, or did or didn't do something. It is exhausting. Men just go on their merry way, dating and having a good time, while women are driving themselves crazy trying to be a psychic, psychiatrist, or mind reader about every little thing he says or does.

Men don't expect other men to talk about much when

they are together. They don't ask each other about their day, what they did at work, or who is dating whom. No, they just want to shoot the breeze with topics like sports, cars, the stock market, and so on.

Men also date up. They have no problem expecting to date a woman with supermodel looks while they themselves could stand to hit the gym and lose fifty pounds. Wouldn't it be fabulous to have the self-esteem of a man? I know that I am speaking to every one of you wonderful ladies out there who are constantly checking yourselves out in the mirror to see if you look fat in your pants. I do the same thing. No man—whether my friend, boyfriend, or husband—has ever asked me if he looks fat or if I like his hair or outfit. Most men are perfectly fine with the way they look. They are what they are, and they go happily about their business of trying to pick up a smoking-hot woman, so much so that they will hold off getting married for years and years until they find exactly what they want. I have had countless male clients who were forty-five plus and had never been married.

On the other hand, women often date down. They think time may be running out to find a husband, or they are lonely, or there aren't many single men left, so they go ahead and date or marry someone with qualities less than they would like. I would urge these women to act like men! Keep your cool and wait for someone to knock your socks off!

Getting Down to the Nitty-Gritty

Dates are supposed to be fun, not a chore, a job, or drudgery. A date is supposed to be about going out and enjoying life and in the process getting to know someone new. So often a date feels like a job interview or an interrogation. What a drag, right?

First dates can be nerve-wracking, considering that your date for the evening will be assessing all of your good points as well as your faults and may find that the latter outweigh the former. The trick is not to worry about whether there will be a second date—just concentrate on having a great first one.

You do want to be attuned to his reactions throughout the time you spend together, however, so that you can accurately assess the situation.

Here are five clues that a man is not interested in you on a date:

1. He is checking out other women in the room or flirting with the waitress.

2. He shows no interest in what you are saying. He has kind of a vacant look in his eyes, like he is in another world.

3. He tells you that he is not interested in a long-term relationship or getting married in the foreseeable future, if ever.

4. He says things that are offensive, sarcastic, or rude. Sometimes a man will use this technique to sabotage a date so that you won't want to see him again.

5. He makes calls on his cell phone throughout the date or is constantly texting.

Being aware of your date's body language or downright blatant clues will help you make a more graceful exit at the end of the evening. Knowing that he isn't really interested actually puts you in the power position of just being able to observe, learn a few things, and know that you will soon be moving on to the next guy and one step closer to finding Mr. Right.

What Your Date Was Really Thinking!

So you went out on a date with a really nice guy. Had a great time, so you thought. He even said that he would like to see you again when you inquired at the end of the date, but then, no call. What happened? Wouldn't you just love to know what your date was really thinking? Did you do something wrong, have spinach in your teeth, bad breath? Do you think you can take it? It could be brutal, after all. The truth is that it doesn't matter how fabulous a person you are. You can be the most beautiful woman on the planet, have a PhD, and speak seven languages, but if you say or do the wrong thing in the beginning stages of dating, you are likely to blow it and never hear from the guy again.

When I was in my twenties (I cringe when I think of how I acted back then), I was constantly saying the wrong thing. I am still known to do that on occasion, but no one is perfect, right? I have always been too honest, and I remember a guy asking me if I liked to ski. I told him no, that I had never tried it and had no interest. He also asked me about several other activities, and I was totally negative about all of them. Looking back, I must have seemed like a total boring drag! Of course, I didn't need to lie and say that I was a champion or anything, but I could have been more interested and told him that I'm not usually into sports, but would love to try everything at least once. That would have made me look a lot more easygoing and fun. I so relate to Oprah Winfrey's comment that she made years ago on her TV show about herself when she was in her twenties. "I weep for the woman I was."

Etiquette Shmetiquette

Here is some feedback from my client Matt about two women he recently met:

"I had dinner with Cari on Tuesday night at La Dolce Vita. We had an enjoyable evening. She seemed interested in me. I invited her to go to the Elton John concert tomorrow night and she seemed happy with that. I sent her a text message after dinner thanking her and have not heard back. I also sent Tatiana a text message more than ten days ago saying that I was happy to be friends and asked her if she wanted to join me at Elton John. I have not heard back either. Not even a courtesy 'no, thank you.' I am beginning to think I am too polite and too much of a gentleman."

I e-mailed Cari and asked her why she did not respond to Matt's text about going to the concert. Her response was, "Marla, I really had a lovely time with Matt; however, I just don't see it working out for us long term. He sent me a text in regard to the concert. I will text him back and let him know that I won't be attending in case there was any confusion about that."

Well, yes! I guess there would be some confusion if she didn't respond either way. She is just not interested, and he is just plain confused.

So many times women just decide to ignore a guy's call or text, hoping that he will "get the hint," but if you have already been out on a date and gotten along well, and he is contacting you for another, then have the courtesy to respond—even if the answer is no. No wonder men get the idea that women are flakes! Believe it or not, men have feelings too. I know that sometimes the only feelings they seem to have are below the belt, but they actually are human and deserve a response.

Again, communication is the key. And speaking of communication, this influx of texting is really confusing things. I would not be surprised in the slightest if one day I hear about a couple getting married by text. People seem to love it that much. The other day a guy told me, "I was actually forced to pay extra to add a texting plan to my cell phone, because people keep texting me and I was getting charged for it anyway."

Whatever happened to picking up the telephone, dialing, and actually speaking to a human being? A text is so impersonal and often doesn't even come through until much later, if at all. I have heard of instances in which people thought they'd been stood up, but the cancellation text from their date never came through. Or the person said they sent a text (who knows if they actually did). Texting can be very convenient, but it has its place. When courting and dating, give the old-fashioned way a try. Pick up the (cell) phone!

A Dozen Ways to Score Points with a Guy

1. Make him and his friends sandwiches for Monday night football.

2. Ditch the flannel pajamas for some silky lingerie.

3. Tell him how adorable he is—often.

4. Stay slim and trim.

5. Laugh at his jokes.

6. Understand when he has to work late and postpone your date.

7. Cook him a special dinner once in a while.

8. Be a good listener.

9. Tivo his favorite shows for him.

10. Have an easygoing attitude—no nagging.

11. Always thank him when he takes you out or does something nice for you.

12. Try to get to know and fit in with his friends and family.

A Dozen Online Dating Dos and Don'ts

Dating online is huge these days. Millions of people are doing it. Some women I talk to about it seem to have a negative feeling about it. They are often concerned that it could be dangerous or a waste of time. I think it can be a great place to meet some wonderful men, since I have personally met many happy couples that connected in just that way. But there are some "rules" that should be followed to make sure that the experience is a pleasant, effective, and safe one.

1. Put up the best and most recent photo of yourself. Men don't focus on what you write as long as they like your photo. Don't use anything too provocative, but don't go too conservative either. I have a friend who put up a photo of herself wearing a business suit; she received very few responses. Show your figure (covered!) and wear a big smile.

2. Less is more when writing your bio. Keep it short and fun. No need to write your whole life story with all of your hopes and dreams. After all, you are a busy woman. You are not sitting home desperate and lonely.

3. Don't initiate the first contact. Answering a man's ad is pursuing him. It is no different from meeting him in a bar or asking him out on a date. Let him initiate and come to you first.

4. Make sure that your sense of humor comes through on your profile and in your messages.

5. Don't even think of misrepresenting your size or age. He will soon find out the truth, and won't that be embarrassing?

6. Make sure that your log-in name is fun and sexy, not marriage-minded or desperate.

7. Always reply to e-mails within a couple of days.

8. Don't volunteer your phone number first.

9. Immediately block anyone who becomes obsessive or annoying.

10. If he doesn't ask you out within four e-mails, delete him and go on to the next.

11. Never e-mail a man a second time if he did not respond to your e-mail.

12. If an e-mail comes with no photo, respond to him that you would love to see a photo. If he refuses, there is a reason—beware.

Don't believe everything a man tells you online. My friend Mae knows a sixty-year-old woman named Lena who was in contact on one of the more popular online dating sites with a much younger man named Simon who lived in London. His photo was gorgeous, and he had a great sense of humor. He charmed, wooed, and flattered her until she believed that they were in love. He told her that he wanted to come and visit her, but he had gone to Nigeria to work and he hurt himself there. He had a big hospital bill and could not leave the country until it was paid. Simon even had the "doctor" call Lena to explain what had happened. Simon said that if Lena would wire a thousand dollars to Nigeria as soon as possible, he would take the next plane and come directly to her house. He wanted to build a life with her and was so excited. She sent him the money and never heard from him again.

When I first heard this story, I thought, how on earth can a mature woman be so naïve? I do understand that some women can fall into a trap because they are so lonely and desperate to be with someone. That is exactly what these type of men prey on. So keep your wits about you. If someone seems too good to be true, or asks you for money, run in the other direction! Also, opening up contact with men in other states or countries is just setting yourself up for heartbreak and frustration. You will be better off finding someone who is geographically desirable.

A Dozen Ways to Make a Guy Run for the Hills

1. Ask him to lend you thousands of dollars.

2. Cry during sex.

3. E-mail him ten times a day.

4. Ask him where you stand as a couple.

5. Talk about what a great lover your ex was.

6. Drink too much at his company party and flirt with his boss.

7. Point out his flaws in front of his friends.

8. Change the programmed radio stations in his car.

9. Read excerpts from your journal to him every night before bed.

10. When he asks you to fix him something to eat, tell him, "You have two hands, make it yourself!"

11. Talk about your biological clock.

12. Try to convert him to your new cult religion.

It's Over—Handling Getting Dumped

It's never fun being dumped, and rarely even satisfying being the dumper, unless you really have an ax to grind.

Nonetheless, both sides of this equation are unpleasant realities of the dating world, so how do you cope when it happens to you? If a major relationship has just ended, then it will understandably take some time to recover. You'll need time to heal and get your game back. If you have only been dating a few weeks or months, it can be empowering to get right back on the horse, as they say.

The most important thing to do is accept what has happened and not try to win your ex back. Come to terms with the loss and know that you will not be single forever.

Don't try to get in touch with him—texting, e-mailing, calling, or any other way—to see if you can work things out. I often get a call or an e-mail from a female client that goes like this: "Hi Marla, I have decided to go back to my ex, so don't match me up anymore, thanks." I want to grab her by the lapels and tell her there is a reason he is her ex and to not even go there! Usually, when this happens, I know that within a few weeks she will be calling me back, saying that it didn't work out and to go ahead and match her up again.

Don't blame yourself. If someone left you, it was his decision and his issue. Clearly, he wasn't "the one" for you. The universe works in mysterious and wonderful ways. You will most likely be thanking a higher power that the sod dumped you and also wishing he'd done it even sooner because when you do meet the right one, everything will become crystal clear.

Do rely on your best friends to comfort you and get you through. Pamper yourself, go out, and do your best to have fun. Remember that life is to be cherished and enjoyed, with or without a man.

Figuring out your weak spots and how people interpret words and actions in the dating arena can only help you be more successful and have a much more pleasant experience overall. Marianne Williamson summed it up beautifully in her book *Enchanted Love,* "The biggest block to love is the human personality."

As little children, we all relate to each other on such a pure and innocent level. We can just be with each other, smile, play, and feel the joy of just being present. When we get older, the ego comes in and makes judgments about the other person. We worry how the other person sees us and what they think of us. Marianne also asks, "Can we love as adults yet reclaim the trust of a child?"

I keep a photo of myself on a shelf near my bed. The photo is of a six-year-old Marla with bright red hair, freckles, and a big smile. I look at that photo every night and remember that little girl's hopes and dreams for the future. The things she used to like to do, the friends she had, the mistakes she made. The benefit to this is knowing deep down that I am still that little girl. When I make mistakes, say the wrong thing, or jump to the wrong conclusion about something, it's okay. Life is about learning and growing. Many years have passed since that photo was taken, but my chances to do it right have not passed. The same is true for everybody! There is *always* a new day and a new opportunity!

Dating Affirmations

I use affirmations on a daily basis in my own life, and the results are remarkable. Taking quiet time for yourself and developing a positive mindset is one of the most powerful life strategies there is. Most of us put ourselves down or compare ourselves negatively to others. Using positive affirmations can change the negative self-talk into something more positive. Keeping your vibration high makes a big difference in attracting wonderful experiences into your life. Here are some affirmations that I find particularly uplifting and powerful. Allow their positive messages to keep you inspired and moving forward.

1. I know that I have the power within me to create a life of fulfillment and joy.

2. Love is all around me. I choose to have love in my life.

3. I am special, unique, and loveable. I love myself unconditionally.

4. The divine plan of my life now takes shape in definite, concrete experiences leading to my heart's desire.

5. The genius within me is now released. I now fulfill my destiny.

6. All doors open for happy surprises, and the Divine plan of my life is speeded up under grace.

7. I know that it is impossible to fail when faith is present.

8. Success, harmony, peace, and confidence are mine.

9. I enjoy life, for each day brings a constant demonstration of the power and the wonder of the universe and myself. I am open to miracles happening daily.

10. I rely on myself. I am powerful and in control.

11. There is no such thing as lack. The universe has infinite supply.

12. The door is always open to admit the positive, the beautiful, the good, and the aspiring.

13. I begin each day with a positive outlook. I intend for wonderful things to happen.

14. I deserve to be loved and know that I am loveable.

15. I live in the now with great expectations for the future.

16. I treat myself with kindness and expect kind treatment from others.

17. I am always open to new ideas. I have an open mind and an open heart.

18. My life is drama-free. I am centered and at peace.

19. The right person for me appreciates my uniqueness and creativity.

20. My heart is open and receptive to a loving relationship. I deserve the best!

Dating Exercise

Create your own affirmations:

1._____

2._____

Good Date, Bad Date

3. _____

4. _____

5. _____

EIGHT

Real-Life Bloopers and Blunders

If indeed you must be candid, be candid beautifully.
                                        —Khalil Gibran

Tales from the Dating Trenches

Here are some actual feedback e-mails I have received from clients after dates. Now, I don't want you to think that these are representative of the majority of e-mails I get, but the fact that I get them at all shows that people are often sending out the wrong messages to their dates and messing up their chances to get into a great relationship. I will never cease to be enlightened, shocked, amused, and amazed in my job as a matchmaker.

Dear Marla,
    Some strange things came up between Ivy and me

and I thought that you might need to know. Prior to meeting Ivy and after a few one-hour conversations we hit it off well. However, during our talks she said she was going to have a new outfit for me for our first date and that it was sexy etc . . .

The day before we were to meet, she texted me a message that the outfit was on hold at the Adidas store and left me the name of the sales rep and his phone number (I guess it was her way of saying buy it for me). No worries, I thought, well, I will just buy it and not look like I am cheap, as I thought what's a hundred or hundred and fifty dollars going to hurt. I called the Adidas store and she had picked out not just an outfit but matching shoes to the tune of almost four hundred dollars. I was completely taken aback but said nothing to her. Ivy came over and we had a fantastic night. I let it go.

Marla, it gets better. Throughout our phone conversations and two dates we talked about travel a lot. I told her that I might be going to Vail for New Year's and Cancun over the holidays. I told her that if things went well between us, maybe she should go with me on one of the trips. She was very receptive to this. A few days later she said that she needed to go to the mall to look for some things. I said that I needed to pick up some sunglasses that I broke and said that I'd meet her down there and afterward we could go next door to P. F. Chang's restaurant. She said great, you can come and see the luggage I am picking out.

With that statement, I came up with a "things changed" and let's meet at my house for Chinese food instead because my meetings were going to run late. She agreed but made sure to leave me the number of the sales rep at Neiman Marcus in the luggage department. I had to confront her politely and tell her that buying fancy and potentially lavish gifts in the very beginning of a relationship can be very confusing and potentially hazardous to someone's feelings. She agreed and seemed okay with it and came over for dinner. It only lasted about an hour and then she came up with "I have to go to the airport to pick up my friend. What time is it? Oh, no, I'm late, gotta go!"

A few days later I got a text message stating that we have different ideas about the future and that we should not see each other again.

Sincerely, Jonathan

I never did give Ivy this feedback, since I am certain she knows exactly what she is doing. I was shocked, however, that this lady is a schoolteacher in San Diego in her early thirties. I usually hear this type of story about the struggling actress/model types in L.A. I felt badly for Jonathan that he had to deal with this type of behavior from someone with whom I matched him.

Hi Marla,

I did go out with Tom on Saturday. He was a nice guy. A gentleman. He expressed that he wanted to go on another date, but he was much too opinionated about food and people for my liking. I'm sure he didn't mean to spit when he talked, but he did. He wanted an answer right then and there about going out again and I didn't give him an answer. Like I said, nice guy but too judgmental for my tastes. I'm sure he'd be perfect for someone who was more conservative.

Annie

This was Jessica's response to my e-mail as to why she hung up on David.

Hi,

David has been calling me since December. From the first conversation with him I was not comfortable. He continued to call me religiously for over one month, sometimes as often as every day. I told him that I was not interested and he continued to call. Finally I just hung up on him.

Jessica

Hi Marla,

Danny is sincere, down-to-earth, and genuine. He has a great heart and excellent manners and has a definite need not to be alone. However, I also found him creepy (he stalked me when I went home for Christmas in Texas and then again when he came to L.A.). He has a habit of calling from a different phone number every time. He didn't seem like the Washington DC type and all and is not worldly in the extreme. Reminded me of Gomer Pyle. I was very surprised upon meeting him that he was nice-looking, well dressed, and chivalrous.

Mitzi

I appreciated Mitzi's honest feedback, however, I would say that she did not know if it was Danny calling her from a differ-

ent number constantly since she did not pick up the phone. She was jumping to conclusions.

Hi Marla,

I did meet Elton. I realized over the phone that he is not that sophisticated, and it was confirmed at dinner. He was tall and nice, but not my type physically. He ate spaghetti with bread, not even asking for a spoon. He was boring and plain. He liked me, held my hand, kissed it, and made compliments. I told him up front at the end of dinner that we could be friends but that I don't have any chemistry with him. He was a bit taken aback by that. He didn't talk to me in the car on the way back. Lesson for me to learn: I will always drive myself in my car to the restaurant. Never again will I let somebody else pick me up from home. Learning from our own mistakes are the best life lessons.

Diana

I got this response from Jennifer when I asked her for feedback on her date with Ryan:

Hey there,

Ryan—get this one, I ordered one roll of sushi to go for my mom and he took my money! It was only ten dollars, but he still took my cash and then he was driving a beater . . . it was like a 1992 red Bronco! He said that he has been renting in San Diego for twelve years or more. I am soooo not interested!

I had to laugh at the way Jennifer expressed herself. Poor Ryan came off as a cheapskate. He really liked her and wanted to see her again.

I spoke to Tara on the telephone today. She had a date with Terrance a few days ago and told me that he had been calling her to set up another date. "Marla, I am really not interested, he was a nice enough guy, good-looking, and we had some laughs, but he told me that his two boys have already been in trouble for smoking pot. That is not the kind of influence that I want around my eleven-year-old son."

This was a case of TMI (too much information) on a first date. There was no reason for Terrance to bring that up so soon. It was a turn-off for Tara. He totally blew it.

One of my clients, Patrick, called me to tell me about his date with a drop-dead gorgeous blonde named Jen. Not only did Patrick find Jen stunning and intelligent, but they also had a ton in common with each other. They both had eight-year-old sons, played golf and tennis, loved wine and travel, and had their pilot's license. Actually, Patrick owned a small plane. For their second date, Patrick invited Jen to fly up to San Francisco from Los Angeles to have a romantic dinner.

Things were going great, but at the end of the dinner, Jen ordered a couple of expensive bottles of wine to take home with her. Of course, Patrick was paying the check. He was stunned that she would be so bold as to do that. He said they went out a couple of more times, but each time she would order the most expensive thing on the menu. He was totally turned off and soon decided not to see her anymore.

I have heard stories like this one over the years. At the end of the first date, the woman would order an extra entrée for herself to be wrapped up and taken home. The men are usually in such shock that they don't say anything, but that is usually the last time they ask her out.

This next feedback is in two parts. The first e-mail is feedback from after the first date, and the second is from after the third.

Hi Marla,
   Thanks for introducing me to Olga. She is sweet and charming and definitely gorgeous. Tall, thin, with striking dark hair, just my type. I would rate her a nine or a ten, for sure! We had a great time talking and laughing. We went to a French restaurant downtown and practically closed the place down. Thanks again.
Tim

Hi Marla,
   I wanted to inform you that I will not be seeing Olga anymore. A few reasons, ones I think will help you going forward looking for me. We were out a total of three times, yesterday being the last time. There was a cultural barrier that was tough to get around. Also, conversation was strained, somewhat "interviewish" most of the time. I was not very relaxed being around her. The chemistry to continue was not there.

And now the guy part in me comes through. I noticed that she did not really "stick out" amongst the ladies at the party downtown we went to Friday night. And yesterday I made two discoveries, which were not pleasing at all. The first was that she had a belly, gut, rolls—there is no nice way to put it. It was hidden well, but at twenty-seven that spells disaster down the road. I know I have work to do after knee surgery, but I know I will get there. And the biggest one of all, she had a hairy upper lip (this is a no-no for me, automatic turn-off!). Dark hair, like a moustache! She does have beautiful features, so I lost that at first. Revised rating, an eight, barely. By the way, I really disliked writing this paragraph. She is a sweet girl and I do feel a bit shallow. I know you do understand though. I hope this helps the whole process of getting to know me better and what I like.

I actually laughed so hard I cried after reading that e-mail. I just didn't know what else to do.

Dear Marla,

Thank you for introducing me to Marina. I have decided not to see her anymore. We had two dates and by date number two I could see red flags all over. She seems to be a very high-society girl who has no trouble spending my money. She is a "gourmet cook and therefore only eats in the finest restaurants." When I offered to take her for a ride on my boat for a picnic with food and a bottle of wine, she responded with "No, daaahling. Only champagne!" Finally, when we kissed good night after each date she would practically suck the tongue out of my mouth, pull away, then dive in again to suck my tongue out . . . strange.

Sincerely, Jake

Initially, Jake e-mailed me with feedback saying that Marina was fabulous and a diva. He was so excited about her, but her high-maintenance attitude quickly turned him off.

I was at my friend Rouben's house last night and he was telling me about a first date he went on with a woman. He took her to a lovely restaurant in Beverly Hills. Things were going fine and she was a great conversationalist. At the end of the meal, she told the waiter that she would like to order one more entrée, to take home to her cat. Rouben's mouth dropped and he said, "Oh, no, I don't think that is a good idea." She replied, "But it is for my cat!" He told her matter-of-factly, "I am not on a date with your cat!"

My husband then told us a story about when he was single and had gone out with a woman a couple of times. One night they were out with his friends and they decided to move the party to one of their homes. They stopped at a 7-Eleven to buy some beer. All of a sudden the woman put a pile of things on the counter to be added to the guys' bill. One of his friends paid for everything. While driving in the car, he reached in the bag and took a piece of chocolate. Well, the woman yelled at him, "How dare you take my chocolate!" My husband slammed on the brakes and gave her an earful. After all, his friend had paid for everything. That was the last date he had with her.

Finally, a cautionary tale—sad but also hilarious—about how drinking too much on a date can be disastrous. This happened to James, a friend of mine who lives in New York. He got involved with a woman named Sarah who lived in Santa Barbara. They really fell for each other and decided to see each other exclusively. James is quite wealthy, so he was able to fly Sarah back east often so that they could spend a lot of time together. He was even thinking about asking her to move in with him. He did, however, notice that she drank a bit too much when they went out and that made him feel a little uncomfortable.

One day, Sarah accompanied James to a convention held in a hotel in Miami that he needed to attend for his business. While he was in a meeting that was to last for a few hours, she went to the bar to wait for him. When he finished his meeting, he went looking for her and found out from the staff that she had gotten so drunk at the bar she was unable to walk. They had to wheel her out on a luggage rack. Well, that was it for James. When they got back to New York, he asked her to pack up her things and he put her on the first plane back to Santa Barbara, never to see her again.

As you can see from the feedback in this chapter, people are confused big time. Hearing bloopers and blunders like these week after week, month after month, and year after year, I sometimes wonder if I should throw in the towel on my matchmaking career. But I take a deep breath and come to the realization that people need and want assistance in figuring it all out, while getting burned as few times as possible along the way.

Now That You've Got Him, Here's How to Keep Him

Now that you've used all of the skills I have taught you, gotten out there, and bagged yourself a soul mate, you want to make sure that your relationship has a winning chance, right? If we look at the statistics, at least 50 percent of you will be getting a divorce. Break-ups and divorces are painful, sad, stressful, difficult, often costly, and just downright crappy!

Some of you might be under the impression that once you find your soul mate, life forever after will be blissful, like in a fairy tale. The two of you will ride off into the sunset and live happily ever after. We human beings are imperfect and tend to forget this fact, especially when we are madly in love with another imperfect human being. We unrealistically expect our relationship to be perfect. I married my soul mate, and we are thrilled to have found each other, but there is plenty of compromise on both sides on a regular basis.

Even while I was writing this book, my husband and I had a few tiffs and I thought, *What am I doing writing a book on how to get into a relationship? I should be writing one on how to avoid it.* (Just kidding!) Cohabitating is stressful, especially if you have lived alone for a long time and are used to doing everything your way. My husband and I had each been living alone for about six years when we met. We were both around forty years old and liked things the way we liked them. I had my own style of decorating, and he had his. It took me a long time to convince him to let me bring all the furniture I wanted to into his place.

His coffee table was completely loaded with knick-knacks, mostly from Mexico. There were little pyramids, animals carved in stone, all kinds of objects completely covering the surface. There was no room to set a cup of coffee down, let alone a book or magazine. I found this very odd, as I always had some coasters, a coffee-table book, and maybe a little Eiffel tower figurine on my coffee table, and that was about it. I did not like his style one bit. When I asked him about it, he said firmly that he liked it that way.

When I went to meet his family in Mexico City and we visited each relative's home (all, by the way, were beautifully decorated), I noticed one common theme. Everyone's coffee table was loaded with knickknacks, beautiful crystal ashtrays, or mostly carvings. Well, that explained everything! It was just cultural, a decorating style he had seen all of his life. He used to say that American rooms with all their empty tables just look silly, while I thought that tables loaded with stuff looked funny. It took a while, but I eventually convinced him to let me move all of the knickknacks into the bedroom in a nice wooden box, which was open and on display.

Then we went shopping and bought a beautiful dark wood coffee table made in South America. It was out first purchase together. What goes on the coffee table might seem minor, but the small things, if not treated with care and respect, can soon mount into big things and turn into problems.

So what are some things that you can do to help ensure that you don't turn out to be one of the statistics? The major issues that newlywed couples often face relate to conflict resolution, finances, in-laws, communication, and sex. A healthy relationship or marriage is filled with honesty and support. It should be joyful, with a sense of familiarity, passion, and comfort.

Studies show that couples that lose the feeling of romance in the first two years of their marriage are more likely to divorce eventually. As a matchmaker, over the years I have had numerous male clients with little kids, infants even, and I've come to realize that this is an especially dangerous time. I am always shocked to meet a man who is divorcing when his wife has barely finished giving birth! The demands of parenthood, work, and everything else that we have to do in life often take a toll on a marriage, and the communication, intimacy, and romance get put on the back burner.

A man needs regular sex and attention to feel loved, needed, and satisfied. If you are not going to provide it, he will look elsewhere—if not right away, eventually. He might not deliberately go out looking for it, but there will come a time when someone at the office starts flirting with him, or when he is out of town on business, and he will justify it by thinking that he isn't getting any attention at home, so why not take advantage of the opportunity? Let your spouse know you care and are thinking about him throughout the day by e-mails, phone calls, and notes. Tell your husband you love him before someone else does!

You must maintain a strong bond and trust, because there are quite a few women out there who are happy to go after another woman's husband. My husband is an entertainer and he tells me all the time that there are women flirting with him, even when they know he is married. He even told me about two of my so-called friends who came on to him while I was out of the room. I am lucky to have a faithful man. He tells me that it is such a pleasure to tell a woman who is flirting with him that he is happily married. But I don't take that for granted. I realize that I need to give him plenty of love and attention, because there are lots of other women who would love to step in.

Remember, ladies, just because you are married or in a relationship, don't trade in your sexy lingerie for sweat pants and a T-shirt with a beer slogan across the chest. Also, most men don't like flannel on a woman. Something silky and feminine is a much better way to keep him happy and interested.

Love and romance are such powerful emotions! Think about how fantastic you felt the last time you had a huge crush on someone or were in love. Love also has consequences for your health and well-being. Engaging in joyful activities such as sharing and giving and receiving love activate areas in the brain responsible for emotion, attention, and motivation. These activities also reduce stress and stimulate health and vitality. The search for a soul mate is the most basic of instincts, the most primal drive in humans. The health of a person's love life has a direct impact on his or her mental and physical health. It is a known fact that married people are healthier than those who are single, divorced, separated, or widowed. And married men live longer than single men.

There are studies that show that sex is more than just physical exercise. Men who have sex at least twice a week are half as likely to die as men who have sex less than once per month. Regular intercourse promotes prostate health for men and estrogen levels in women, which help to keep the heart healthy. Making love can also help you stay young-looking. It is thought to reduce the external signs of aging caused by stress. What a bonus! Love might have its ups and downs, but purely from a health and well-being perspective, it's well worth it.

Quality time together is crucial. Don't let your job, friends, or the kids interfere with your marriage. If you are both busy, here are some ideas to get in some quality time:

1. Schedule a date night once a week or every other week. Do something special and fun, just the two of you.

2. Take showers together. You are guaranteed alone time there!

3. Clean the house together, fold laundry, wash the car, go grocery shopping. It might not sound too glamorous or fun, but the time spent together is more important than the activity.

4. Work out together. I used to spend money on a personal trainer; now my husband is my trainer. Every Saturday we go to the gym for an hour. I get to spend time with him, and my abs are getting tighter.

5. If you have kids, make a deal with another couple to exchange childcare, so you can both have evenings out.

Learning to fight fair is a crucial part of a successful relationship. Just because you have found your soul mate doesn't mean that you won't have any arguments. Some big, some small, but they are guaranteed to come up, and when they do, it is important that they not tear your relationship apart. If you fight fair, disagreements can actually strengthen a marriage.

Here are ten rules to stick to when fighting fair:

1. No name-calling.

2. Don't bring up past history; stick to the issue at hand.

3. Keep the argument between the two of you; don't involve family members, girlfriends, or your kids.

4. Don't interrupt each other. Take turns expressing your feelings and listening to each other.

5. Speak in a normal tone. No yelling or screaming. People tune out when the volume is turned up.

6. Don't go to bed angry. Even if you don't see eye to eye on a subject, forgive and call a truce before going to sleep.

7. Don't argue in a public place. Keep it private.

8. Tell your partner how you feel rather than putting the blame on him.

9. If you can, hold hands during the fight, and keep eye contact.

10. Even if you are really angry, remember the things that you love about him. No one is perfect! Emphasize the positive aspects of your relationship. Don't focus on the negative. Always look for the best in each other. When you met your partner, you fell in love with all of his wonderful qualities. Create a list of all the things you love about him and remind yourself of these traits—often.

Remember that men have a need to be right, and also a need to protect their woman. Women don't realize this, and often arguments and hurt feelings occur when a woman tries to tell a man what to do. Men are raised to be tough, never cry, and know what to do in every situation. Men feel that not being able to do something or to solve a problem means that they are a failure as a man. That's the reason men never want to stop and ask for directions—they don't want another man solving their problem. (Thank goodness we now have navigation systems!)

Women should avoid saying anything to a man that will make him feel like he is wrong. Praise your man for everything he does right instead of telling him all of the things that he is doing wrong. He will feel proud and happy to be with you. I remember one Thanksgiving years ago when I was married to a chef. My dad was trying to carve the turkey but having a heck of a time with it. I suggested letting my husband do it, since he was a professional. My dad refused, I kept mentioning it, and my dad became more and more aggravated. I later realized that by suggesting that he was not capable of carving a turkey, it was a blow to his capabilities as a man.

The old saying "The way to a man's heart is through his stomach" still holds true, even in today's modern world when women are out there busting their buns just as hard as the men. A man loves to see his woman's domestic side, and a home-cooked meal made with love scores big points. You don't have be a gourmet cook, but showing that you care and are capable of making him a nice meal or entertaining some friends is important. I have heard some men say they don't date American women anymore because they don't take care of their man like the women do in certain other cultures. They don't want to hear "You've got two hands, make it yourself!" when they ask for something to eat.

The other day my husband was complaining that I never make him coffee in the morning. I told him that because he is still asleep when I leave for work in the morning, it had never even crossed my mind. He said I could make it so it would be ready for him when he wakes up. He likes the idea that his wife is taking care of him in that way. I have always had a hard time keeping up with the demands of a full-time career and taking care of a home while married. In Mexico, my sisters-in-law and cousins all have maids. My husband's sister has two live-in maids and another one who comes twice per week, and that is for a family of three! A maid in Mexico earns twenty dollars per day, all day—and they cook too!

I just can't justify spending three times that amount of money to have a maid here, so I scramble around as fast as I can to keep up. I think it will always be unbalanced as far as what men expect from us; we'll always be "doing it all." Even though my husband helps out a lot with the housework, I still feel the pressure of most of it falling on me if things are not done. Traditional roles still hold in our society, even though they have become a bit blurred.

One last thing about our domestic side! I am laughing so hard I am crying right now. While I was writing today, I was also doing the laundry. My husband used to want to do the laundry, but I took that job away from him since he crammed so many clothes into one load that I couldn't see how they could get clean. He insisted that he had been trained by his maids while growing up and knew how to do laundry like a professional, and I didn't. Well, that didn't fly with me, so I took over the job.

But, as I explained to my husband, in this country we have a problem with our socks: they disappear in the dryer. I don't know what to do about it, but all of the women in the United States have the same problem. While I was waiting for a second load to dry, I laid out some of the laundry on the bed from the previous load. My husband came over to my desk with seven different socks fanned out in his hands. "What in the heck is this?" he asked. "Where are my socks?" I replied, "I am so sorry, I have no idea. I checked the washer and dryer thoroughly. I just don't understand what happens to the socks!" Then he said something in Spanish that I won't repeat and walked away. I guess I will be buying him some more socks today.

The heart of a healthy, successful marriage is a deep friendship. Two people who have a deep respect for each other and sincerely enjoy each other's company have the best chance for success. Also, create a spiritual connection. A couple can grow closer when they share some form of spirituality. You have probably heard the saying "The family who prays together, stays together." It's true!

In a happy and healthy marriage, you will find two people committed to making each other happy. The wife respects and trusts her husband, and the husband cherishes his wife and puts her needs above his own. We live in a very selfish society presently. Recently, here in Los Angeles, there was a controversial billboard advertisement for a divorce attorney. It said something like, "Life is too short, get a divorce." I was also shocked to hear of a new website being advertised on a local radio station. When I heard the ad for the first time, my mouth actually hung open. It is a dating website for people "already in a relationship but wanting something more." No wonder we have a sky-high divorce rate! There seem to be challenges at every turn. But you can be the exception to the rule. You can have a fulfilling and wonderful relationship that others will admire and aspire to.

NINE

Dating Q & As: Ask Marla

Love doesn't make the world go 'round; love is what makes the ride worthwhile.

—Franklin P. Jones

How long should I wait to introduce the man I am seeing to my children?

It is best not to introduce anyone you have been dating seriously for less than six months to your children. At the start of dating, regardless of how well things seem to be going or how excited you are, you really don't know if this particular romantic interest is going to work out long term. Your children have already had to deal with their family breaking up; the last thing they need is a parade of men coming in and out of their lives. Also, think of how awkward it would be if you wanted to get rid of the guy, but the kids have taken a liking to him, or if they don't like him and you really do. You need to put your children before your own life. Keep your promises to your kids. You chose to have children; now you must take the responsibility and put dating and men second place.

What if he's not marriage material now, but I can see the potential?

Forget it, ladies! Find a man who already has the qualities you are looking for. Now, I am not saying that if you are both young and he is still getting an education and will be moving up in his career, that you should not be with him. I am talking about situations like he is forty and still living with his parents or has roommates and smokes pot all day; when he's still trying at fifty to get that record deal while he expects you to support him—well, you get the idea. If you are fine with those scenarios or something similar, then that is all right, but if not, move on to someone who already has something going on. Don't think that with your encouragement or advice that he will change into what you want him to be. So many women are so eager to fall in love and get married that they give a guy credit for qualities that he doesn't have and won't ever develop. Don't fall for a guy until you know all that you need to about him. You want a man with good character and the qualities that are important to you now, not possibly someday.

Don't commit to or marry a guy if:

• He is jealous and it has been an issue in his past relationships.

• He abuses drugs or alcohol. An addict will always give priority to his addiction. You cannot save him or change that; the desire to change has to come from within him.

- He is gay and you think that you can change him.

- He tries to isolate you and makes you give up your friends and activities that you enjoy.

- He makes fun of you or tells you that you are stupid.

My fiancé and I recently broke up after a three-month engagement. Can I keep the ring?

Here are the rules on keeping the ring: If the split was your idea, then you should return the ring. If the split was his idea, then you can keep the ring. If the ring belonged to his grandmother or is a family heirloom, then the ring should be returned to his family.

The guy I'm dating hasn't yet said, "I love you." Should I tell him first?

No, don't be the one to say those words first. Once you say it, it's out there, and if he doesn't return the sentiment, oh, boy, will things be awkward from then on. If it has been more than six months and he can't say, "I love you," then consider moving on. Don't waste your time. Chances are that if he can't tell you he loves you, he won't marry you either.

How much do cultural differences matter?

Cultural differences can sometimes turn out to be a big deal. When I was twenty-five and working in a French restaurant, one of the waiters, Philippe from Nice, took a liking to me. We went out as friends and I liked being with him and practicing my French. One day he told me that he had romantic feelings for me and wanted to take our relationship to the next level. I had to say no because, although he was very sweet and sexy, he had told me on another occasion that when he would be married one day, he planned to have a mistress. He said that his father always had a mistress and he planned to do the same. Well, that cultural difference was a deal-breaker for me.

When getting involved with someone from another country or culture, it is a good idea to find out what their customs or expectations are when it comes to romantic relationships, marriage, and possibly raising children so that you can make sure you are both on the same page and comfortable with each other's lifestyle and values.

We've been dating a year, but he's still not making a commitment. Should I stick it out? I really want to get married.

If you have been dating a man for a year and he still doesn't want to be exclusive, you are looking at a problem. If you have been dating exclusively for a year, but he just hasn't proposed, don't sweat it if things are going smoothly. Sometimes the relationship has to grow. A year is not really that long. It actually gives you the chance to really get to know someone and decide whether you want to spend your entire life with him.

He says he doesn't want more kids. I think I can change his mind, though. Should I risk it?

As I mentioned before, don't ever think that you are going to change someone. Having children is a huge commitment, and if the person you are thinking of getting involved with is not on the same page as you, then either accept it or move on. I have heard of women getting pregnant even though the man told her that he didn't want more kids, or trying to trap a man into getting married because they are pregnant. What a disaster that is. The man feels betrayed and resentful, the relationship will most likely end, and our society has another child from a broken home.

It seems like everyone is just too busy to date. Are guys really serious these days about finding the right person?

I am asked this question a lot. Men will come in and join the matchmaking service I work for and pay an exorbitant amount of money for me to find them a wife, but then they don't seem to have the time to really develop a relationship. In some cases, they're too busy even to meet anyone! Their heart is in the right place—they really would like to have someone in their life—but oftentimes the men, just like us ladies, are working so darn hard and so many hours that it seems impossible to find the time to cultivate a real relationship. Many men who come to me own several companies and are flying all over the world doing business. That means that dating gets put on the back burner. So my answer to this is, yes, everyone wants to be with their soul mate, but, unfortunately, society and making a good living have preoccupied many of us with just that.

I also want to point out that if you are on a date with a man and you seem to be getting along great, but he mentions how busy he is and that he is not really interested in getting married or involved anytime soon, it most likely means that he is not interested in you in a romantic way. This is his way out of committing to seeing you again or getting involved.

Also, cutting to the chase with a guy right up front is a huge turn-off. Women tend to obsess about marriage whether they are dating anyone or not. And when they meet a guy, they immediately go into the thought mode of: Is he the one? Getting into a serious relationship is always at the forefront of their minds. When it comes to dating, take your time and see if this guy is worth a second, third, or fourth date. See whether you are even compatible before jumping ahead into a marriage-minded frenzy.

Is it a good idea to ask a man out? Is it true that men like to be the one to pursue?

Conventional wisdom says, "It's the man's job to do the pursuing," but in the modern world we can nudge them along a little bit. Guys have a tough deal: always having to pursue, and getting rejected a good deal of the time. I think that if a man is showing some interest, you can go ahead and try one of these techniques. Don't actually use the word "date" or "go out with me." You don't want to sound too serious. You can always say something like "I'm going to be in your area for a meeting, would you like to meet for a drink?" A drink can turn into a dinner or a whole evening if things are going well.

You can also ask him for advice. If he is a computer

whiz, for example, or knows a lot about cars and you are in the market to buy one, then you can always offer to buy him a drink for his help. Subtlety is the key. I don't suggest coming on like a man and flat out asking him for a date. You can suggest doing something together without seeming like you are the aggressor or chasing him. I still believe that the man likes the challenge and the hunt, and if it comes too easy, he might lose interest quickly. A man is biologically hardwired to do the chasing. And as far as who pays for what, if the man asked you out, then let him pay. If you suggest an outing, then you should pay.

I've been told I am too honest. Isn't it good to speak your mind and let a man know what your opinion is on things?

These days, women are more educated, independent, and opinionated than at any other time in history. We love to speak our minds. Men appreciate an intelligent lady, but they also still enjoy being the man and giving advice and help to their woman. My husband loves the fact that I am intelligent and successful, but he still loves to play the traditional role of the man in our relationship. "I'm the man of the house," he proudly tells me. That means he wants to watch out for me, make important decisions, and give me advice—not so much the other way around. It is important for a man to know that his advice and opinion are respected and listened to. As for women, it's okay not to sound off on everything that comes to mind.

I've had three dates with a guy and he just asked me to go to Vegas with him for the weekend. I'm not comfortable sleeping with him yet. How do I handle the room situation?

My opinion is, don't travel with a man unless you are going to sleep together. Even if he gets you your own room, it's not worth the risk of feeling the pressure, being uncomfortable, arguing with him, or feeling guilty about his expenditures without him getting the bonus of sex. Tell him that you prefer to get to know him better before taking trips together.

I was recently in a situation where I was going to be intimate with someone new, but neither of us had a condom. I am worried that a guy might think I am loose if I carry condoms with me. What is the best solution?

Your health is the most precious thing you have. One night of incredible sex is never worth contracting a disease. If you find yourself in the situation where neither of you has a condom, do not be pressured to go ahead and do it anyway. If a man respects you, he would never put you at risk or make you feel uncomfortable. If you are single, it is important to be prepared and be responsible. Don't be concerned with what he might be thinking—the important thing is that you are thinking of yourself!

I think I'm too old to get out there and date again, but I don't want to be alone forever. What can I do?

Some people subscribe to the idea that dating is for young people. Let me assure you, that could not be further from the truth. Love has no age limit! My aunt met her fiancé at the age of fifty-seven. She had been married for thirty years when my uncle died. She eventually decided that she didn't want to be alone, so she went on Match.com and met a great guy while in her early fifties. They had a three-year relationship, then when that didn't work out, she went back online and met her current fiancé. He is a wonderful man and they couldn't be happier together.

After an eighty-six-year-old man's wife passed away, I matched him to a wonderful woman, and they are happy as clams. He is quite wealthy and theirs is an amazing lifestyle of travel and enjoying life. Sure, it's more challenging after a certain age to find someone with whom you can really get along, but there is no reason to believe that there is an age limit on love or companionship. Stay active, curious, keep your look current, try to stay out of the larger sizes, and you can catch a man's eye at any age!

I have heard that guys like to chase a woman and are more interested in a woman that is in demand. Is this true?

I have a female client named Dori. She is very sexy, sweet, down-to-earth, and successful. Men really like her, and I very much want to help her find the right one. I have introduced her to several men over the last few months. They were all interested in her and wanted to see her again, but they also all told me that Dori makes no bones about letting them know she is actively dating and has a lot of guys after her. She was seeing one guy named Carl for a couple of months. They really liked each other and were having a lot of fun. Carl told me that he would like to be exclusive with her, but he knew that she was dating a lot of other guys as well, and it didn't seem like she was planning to settle down. He was getting turned off and eventually stopped calling her and decided to move on. When I told Dori that a few guys had mentioned that she tells them right off the bat she is dating a lot and is in high demand, she was surprised and didn't seem to understand what I was talking about. She said to me, "I liked Carl the best, so it is odd that he would not call me. I feel like giving up on these men." Dori didn't realize that she was turning men off by revealing too much about her dating life. She wanted to seem attractive and in demand, but it actually scared the men away.

Men do like a chase, but they don't want to feel like they are in a stable of guys a woman is keeping. The way to be mysterious and have a guy enjoy chasing you is just to be busy living your life. You don't always have to be available at the drop of a hat. Don't sleep with him too soon, and let him know that you have a lot of interests, but you do not have to mention other men.

I have heard that it is not a good idea to date someone you work with. I have a crush on a coworker. What's the harm?

A large number of people do meet and date through work. After all, we spend at least eight hours a day with people we are paid to be with in a place that we often daydream about leaving. I have heard that more people die on Monday mornings than any other time. You often hear people exclaiming "TGIF!" (Thank God it's Friday). Five o'clock, especially five o'clock on Friday, is often employees' favorite time of the day. If you are not fortunate enough to own your own business or be utterly passionate about your job at the office, a little excitement and diversion can be extremely attractive. That hot guy who works down the hall or in the next cubicle, or your manager at the restaurant where you work suddenly catches your eye, you start flirting, then go out after work for a drink with the gang that turns into drinks alone after work, and then . . . well, you get the picture. Work becomes more exciting, and you no longer dread going in but actually get excited deciding what to wear each day.

All of that is just dandy until it all goes terribly wrong. Now, some of you reading this are currently either seeing someone happily from the office or have done so in the past with no repercussions. Thank your lucky stars, because it is all too easy for things to go the other way. If it doesn't work out between you, life at work can get very uncomfortable. You will once again be watching that clock for quitting time! Or even worse, you could lose your job.

When I was in my early twenties, I was a hostess at a restaurant in West Hollywood. I starting dating the manager, Richard, and eventually we moved in together. I had worked there for three and a half years and really liked it. Dating the manager caused problems with the other employees. Richard was extremely jealous. I became friends with one of the waitresses, who was French. I was learning French and felt very happy to be included in her circle of French friends. Sometimes she would invite me to a party or to hang out with her group. Richard had no interest in going to these parties with me, so I would go without him. Richard was convinced that Nathalie was introducing me to French guys, so he threatened to fire both of us. I was distraught because not only was that not true, but why should she be fired because I was dating a lunatic? Because she was from France and her papers were expiring, it would not be easy for her to find another job. I felt I had to tell her about Richard's threats. Of course, she panicked, was completely stressed, and our friendship was on the line. The whole thing was a horrible mess. (Nathalie moved back to France the next year and I am happy to say that we are still the best of friends more than twenty years later.)

When Richard and I split up, he fired me. I was already devastated and completely stressed out over the breakup and having to find a new place to live. Then I found myself with no job as well. The whole relationship was a disaster from beginning to end.

The problem with dating at work is that you are bringing powerful feelings and emotions to a place that should be your safe haven from everything emotional. So my opinion on dating where you work is simple: DON'T.

I dated a guy for about a month and it didn't work out. We decided to become friends and now he has a new girlfriend who is jealous. She texted me, telling me to leave him alone. I have only known him for a few months, but we get along great. What should I do?

This can be a sticky situation. Jealousy is not an attractive trait, and if she continues this type of behavior, he might say adios to her in the near future. But unless or until that happens, it is best that you take a step back and just leave him alone to develop his relationship. If you care for him as a friend, then you want him to have the best chance at making it work with her. He is not a lifelong friend, so it shouldn't be a big deal to leave it alone.

How do I tell a guy that I don't want to see him again?
Unfortunately, chemistry is not negotiable. Even if he seems perfect on paper and your mother would love him, if you don't feel the chemistry for romance, it's not going to work. If he is a really great guy and you enjoy spending time with him, you can always turn him into a friend. Be diplomatic about telling him—you don't want to hurt his feelings or bruise his ego. You can just tell him that you realize that since there aren't a lot of romantic sparks, you two will probably end up being great friends. Help him to understand that you are not rejecting him, but be clear and firm about the way you feel. I think it's charming to say, "Chuck, I wish that I could sprinkle some chemistry dust over us because you are such a great guy, but I would love to be friends!"

I had an amazing date with a guy. We even kissed a few times and he really seemed to be into me, but now he isn't calling me. Why do guys do this?
I know it can be very confusing when a guy seems to be into you and then pulls back. But the cold/hard facts are that just because a guy kisses you or even sleeps with you does not mean that he has any intention of getting into a relationship with you. Guys want sex, so even if a girl is not everything he is looking for, he is fine with just having fun for the night, a week, or even a few months. Unfortunately, once a woman is intimate with a man, that darn oxytocin

kicks in and makes you get attached. In women, oxytocin is released during hugging, touching, and orgasm. It is often referred to as the hormone of love. That is why it is much more difficult for a woman to date like a guy and love 'em and leave 'em.

Am I a job snob? I met a sexy, funny guy at a party recently. We really hit it off and saw each other for breakfast the next day and a movie the next night. He finally told me what he does for a living. He wears a character costume outside different businesses. I don't want to be shallow, but I was turned off immediately.

What someone chooses to do for a living tells you a lot about the person. Although it is important to see everyone for who they are and appreciate their inner qualities and not just what they do for work, you also have to be aware of the choices men you date are making. If he has this job because he is lazy and doesn't want to put in the effort to get educated or find a real career, then this can be a problem. Also, is someone who has an extremely low-paying job with no benefits going to be able to be there financially for his family and kids? On the other hand, if he is dressing up in silly costumes just to make it though a rough patch while he is looking for work or going to school, then it is admirable that he isn't above doing what he has to do to get things in order and pay his bills.

Men often have preconceived ideas about women with certain professions. I have had men tell me that they would not want to date a lawyer because they feel that she would have too strong a personality. I have also had men tell me that they would not want to date a massage therapist or a hairdresser because they feel that she would not have anything in common with his high-powered lifestyle in the business world. Personally, I bless all of you massage therapists and hairdressers because I don't know what I would do without you!

I have been dating a guy for two months. We get along great, but he has never introduced me to any of his friends or family. When I ask him about it, he changes the subject. Should I be concerned?

You should absolutely be concerned. If a man refuses to include you in his personal life in this way, it is a huge red flag. Either he is seeing another woman as well or is married, gay, or ashamed of dating you, or there is some other reason that you might never find out. None of these scenarios are acceptable, so if he doesn't come clean on why he is avoiding it, my advice is to move on.

I have been dating my boyfriend for six months and he wants to move in together. I am a little apprehensive. If I move in, maybe he won't marry me. What should I do?

Men have a problem with monogamy today because women have made it so easy for them! Remember the old saying "Why buy the cow if you can get the milk for free?" I do agree with the idea of having an engagement ring before moving in together. Keeping your own place and independence is a motivator for a man to "seal the deal" and make it official. If it is a bit inconvenient for him when he wants to see you or spend the night with you, it will move him much quicker toward making a commitment. I have heard countless tales of women living with a man who keeps putting off the wedding day until finally the woman gets fed up, kicks the guy out, and then watches him marry someone else only months later.

I went out with a guy twice and we had an amazing time, but now he is not calling me. Should I call him?

The calling game is the most frustrating thing about dating. You had such a great time, but then don't hear anything, so your mind starts imagining all sorts of scenarios. Maybe he lost your number, maybe he had to go out of town on an emergency, maybe he got in a car crash and is in a coma somewhere (my personal favorite!). But alas, the guy always turns out to be alive and well. Absolutely do not call him. If a guy wants to see you again, he will call you. If he is not calling, that means that he is not interested. You might have had an amazing time together, but for some reason he doesn't feel that you two are suited for each other for the long term. He might have been dating someone else as well and decided to see her exclusively. Whatever the reason, he isn't calling, so leave it at that. Keep your options open and see what's out there. Enjoy the dating process.

Where is this going?

As usual, I listened to the radio on my way home from work tonight. I like to listen to a controversial shock jock named Tom Leykis. You either love him or hate him. He tells it like it is about men and women. One thing he said tonight reminded me of when I was single and dating like it was a second job. He was saying how annoying it is when a woman wants to know "Where is this going?" I say in my book *Excuse Me, Your Soul Mate Is Waiting*, "If you have to ask a guy, 'Where is this going?' it is going nowhere." I remember asking a guy I was dating that very question. He called me every day, had a key to my apartment, and slept over regularly. I foolishly asked him where things were going, and I got a reality check, slap in the face, kick in the stomach, whatever you want to call it. He said, "Oh, no, you are not my girlfriend. I am not ready for a girlfriend."

Men can easily compartmentalize love, sex, relationships, and friendships, whereas women take any attention to mean that this guy is our soul mate. Men need sex. Men want sex. Men want to see naked women. Don't confuse this with "He wants to marry me and have babies!"

Ladies, beloveds, go out and have fun. Date, experience, take the dinners, the shoes, the compliments, live your life. It's okay if every guy you accept a dinner date with is not your soul mate. If he doesn't call, that's okay. You are exciting, you are precious, you are ready for the next adventure. You know where this is going? This is the direction of your life, and it is going in the *right* direction!

Dating Journal

Love does not consist of gazing at each other, but in looking together in the same direction.

 —Antoine de Saint-Exupéry

As they say, you sometimes have to kiss a lot of frogs to find that prince. With the skills you have now learned, it is to be hoped that those slimy kisses will be kept to a minimum. Make several copies of the following two pages so that you always have some on hand. Use this journal to keep track of your dates and help you stay on course on the road to happily-ever-after. Fill it out after each first date and track your progress as time goes by.

Day and time of date:

_____

Name of the lucky gentleman:

_____

How we met:

_____

Where we went on first date:

_____

Initial impression of him:

_____

Was there chemistry?	Yes	No
I did most of the talking:	Yes	No
He did most of the talking:	Yes	No
The conversation flowed smoothly:	Yes	No
He was a gentleman:	Yes	No

The qualities that I liked most about him were:

_____

I was proud of myself for:

_____

Did he ask me for another date?   Yes   No

Would I see him again?   Yes   No

Was the time I spent with him worth it?   Yes   No

The best thing about the date was:

_____

The worst thing about the date was:

_____

The one and only reason that you are unhappy is that life is not happening the way you think it should happen. There are two aspects to this. One is you can go about fixing your life to concur with your thoughts, or the kind of thought that you need. If your happiness and your well-being are not subject to anybody or anything, only then are you free. Otherwise, whether you are in prison or walking on the street, you are still a prisoner within yourself.

—*Sadhguru Jaggi Vasudev,* Midnights with the Mystic

About the Author

Marla was born in Tacoma, Washington, the "City of Destiny." Born with a natural flair for acting, she also had a deep interest in reading and writing poetry and short stories. At the age of sixteen, she was living in Iran with her family and learning to speak French and Persian. During the revolution in Iran, Marla's family moved back to Washington, where she finished her last year of high school and one year of college.

After that, she moved to Hollywood to pursue an acting career, doing television commercials and print modeling. In the early 1990s, she moved to Chicago where she found that she could use her dating experience to help others. She has been working in Los Angeles as a matchmaker since 2001 and has successfully introduced many couples that have gotten married!

Marla's work inspires people and gives them hope that they can find their soul mate. Marla married her own in Mexico City in 2002. A world traveler and culture nut, Marla describes herself as having a French flair, a Persian heart, Italian fire, and Mexican taste buds!

Hampton Roads Publishing Company

. . . for the evolving human spirit

bettie youngs books

HAMPTON ROADS PUBLISHING COMPANY publishes books
on a variety of subjects, including spirituality,
health, and other related topics.

For a copy of our latest trade catalog, call toll-free,
800-766-8009, or send your name and address to:

HAMPTON ROADS PUBLISHING COMPANY, INC.
1125 STONEY RIDGE ROAD • CHARLOTTESVILLE, VA 22902
e-mail: hrpc@hrpub.com • www.hrpub.com